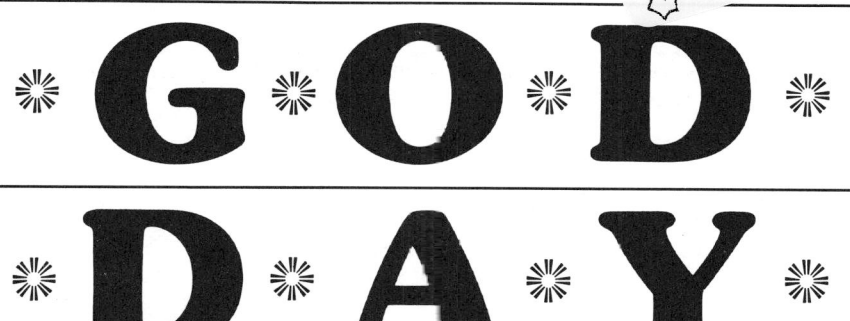

GOD DAY BY DAY

FOLLOWING THE WEEKDAY LECTIONARY

VOLUME FOUR

ADVENT AND CHRISTMAS

COMMENTARY ON THE TEXTS
SPIRITUAL REFLECTIONS ✹ SUGGESTED PRAYERS

MARCEL BASTIN · GHISLAIN PINCKERS · MICHEL TEHEUX
TRANSLATED BY DAVID SMITH

Paulist Press • New York/New Jersey

Originally published under the title *Dieu Pour Chaque Jour (4)* copyright © 1982 by Editions Desclée, Paris. English translation copyright © 1985 by The Missionary Society of St. Paul the Apostle in the State of New York.

All rights reserved. No part of this book may be reproduced or transmitted in any form or by any means, electronic or mechanical, including photocopying, recording or by any information storage and retrieval system without permission in writing from the Publisher.

Library of Congress
Catalog Card Number: 84–60391

ISBN: 0–8091–2699–0

Published by Paulist Press
997 Macarthur Boulevard
Mahwah, New Jersey 07430

Printed and bound in the
United States of America

CONTENTS

Presentation 1
Introduction 2

THE ADVENT SEASON:
FROM THE MONDAY OF THE FIRST WEEK
TO THE WEDNESDAY OF THE SECOND WEEK:
THE SEASON OF THE FUTURE

Isaiah, the Prophet of Advent

Monday 1	At the Heart of the World	10
Tuesday	Crazy Hope	13
Wednesday	The Banquet of the Poor	15
Thursday	An Impregnable City	17
Friday	The Death of the Tyrants	19
Saturday	The Stars, the Sun and Good News	21
Monday 2	The Wasteland Will Bloom	24
Tuesday	The God of Tenderness	26
Wednesday	A Light Burden	28

FROM THE THURSDAY OF THE SECOND WEEK
TO THE FRIDAY OF THE THIRD WEEK:
THE TIME OF THE FORERUNNER

The Bridegroom's Friend

Thursday 2	In Praise of Violence	31
Friday	Join in the Game!	33
Saturday	A Whirlwind of Fire	35
Monday 3	The Authority of the Spirit	37
Tuesday	A Little Remnant	39
Wednesday	The Scandal of the Gospel	41
Thursday	Passionate Love	43
Friday	Indirect Lighting	46

THE OCTAVE BEFORE CHRISTMAS:
THE TIME OF GIVING BIRTH

The Infancy Gospels: Symbol or Reality?

December 17	The New Man	50
December 18	Emmanuel	52
December 19	Barren Women	54
December 20	The House of Silence	57
December 21	Springtime Dance	60
December 22	A Canticle for a Revolution	62
December 23	God Is Gracious	64
December 24	Give Voice to Praise	66

THE SEASON OF CHRISTMAS

THE FIRST EPISTLE OF JOHN

BETWEEN CHRISTMAS AND THE NEW YEAR:
WITNESSES TO THE LIGHT

December 26	A Child Challenging Death (Saint Stephen)	76
December 27	A Glance—a Word (Saint John)	80
December 28	Solidarity with Exiles (the Holy Innocents)	83
December 29	The Encounter	86
December 30	The Old World Has Passed Away	88
December 31	Alpha and Omega	90

BETWEEN THE NEW YEAR AND THE EPIPHANY:
THE BOOK OF VOCATIONS

January 1	Solemnity of Mary, Mother of God	95

January 2	He Came in Our Flesh 99
January 3	The Holy One of God 103
January 4	Fascination 106
January 5	Open-hearted Love 110
January 6	Heaven Is Open 113
January 7	Wine at the Wedding 114

THE WEEK AFTER THE EPIPHANY: THE MANIFESTATIONS OF THE WORD

Monday	Light at the Crossroads 118
Tuesday	Loving Is Knowing 120
Wednesday	Beyond Fear 124
Thursday	Today 128
Friday	Water and Blood 130
Saturday	Perfect Joy 133

CELEBRATING THE SAINTS' DAYS THROUGHOUT THE YEAR

PRESENTATION

This book is another in a set of books embracing the whole of the Church's weekday lectionary. Many books have already appeared containing commentaries, suggestions and prayers for the Sundays of the three-year cycle of readings. We have been waiting for the initiative to be taken to provide books for the weekdays similar to those already in existence for Sundays and now we have an addition to the new series.

The structure and method of presentation are quite straightforward. The authors have followed the order of the days of the week, but have grouped certain days together according to liturgical periods or within homogeneous wholes, each of which is preceded by an introductory note.

Under each day, the following three elements will be found:

1. A short commentary on the readings and the Psalm. A biblical expert has drawn a clear, simple and firmly based message from the sacred texts.

2. A spiritual text, intended to provide material for private meditation, preparation for the homily and other purposes outside the Eucharist itself, both by individuals and by groups.

3. Suggestions for prayer, which can be used to extend meditation, for example, by thanksgiving. These prayers can also be used throughout the rest of the day. Their language and thought are strongly biblical.

The authors do not intend any of these three elements to be used to replace the texts and prayers of the liturgy itself. The very reverse is true—because the authors' aim is to help the reader to prepare for and to extend the liturgical act, their suggestions are above all at the service of the liturgy. They have their origin in the Eucharist and their only intention is to help to make each day holy. To that end, these suggestions are an attempt to stimulate the spiritual benefits of the liturgy to flow as from a source of life-giving water.

The Editor

THE VOLUMES IN THIS SET

Lent and Easter
Ordinary Time: Matthew
Advent and Christmas

These books are the result of ministry and pastoral experience in the parish of Saint-Denis in Liège, Belgium. The parish church is at the center of a neighborhood that is dominated by trade, administration and leisure, and the local community that has grown up there is always in a state of movement. The church is visited every day by a very great number of people living and working there. It is that aspect of the church that the authors have also tried to present in the pages that follow.

INTRODUCTION

We have outlined some of the ways in which the books in this series can be used in Volume 1 (Lent and Easter). In this volume, we deal with Advent and Christmas and some of the most important saints' days.

The biblical and liturgical interest in Advent and Christmas is not difficult to discern. Whole sections of Scripture are read only during this liturgical season: the prophet Isaiah, the infancy gospels and the first chapter of John, to mention only a few. This book contains substantial introductions to these biblical books and a day-to-day commentary on the texts taken from them for use in the liturgy. The readings also lead us to reflect deeply about the meaning of what have for a very long time been called the "theological virtues"—faith in Jesus Christ, Son of God and true man, the hope that forms an integral part of the messianic message of the Bible, and the charity—the agape or love—that of the theological message of the Apostle John. We have, in other words, tried to show that this liturgical season is not intended simply to provide a sentimental prelude to and celebration of Christmas with a strong admixture of folklore. On the contrary, our aim has been to reveal some of its infinite riches.

Toward the end of the book several pages are devoted to saints' days. Our celebration of the saints flows traditionally from our celebration of Christ's incarnation, since the Lord continues his history on earth in his holy people. It is therefore valuable to offer to readers a few aspects of this great adventure in which the Church has always been involved at every period of its existence and which can be seen in the lives of our brothers and sisters, the saints.

THE ADVENT SEASON

"Tell me, what do you hope for?"

"Strongest of all is hope!"—and Joan of Arc dies, burnt by the fire of love (Honegger's Oratorio "Joan at the Stake"). If we are really immersed in God's word in this season of Advent, hope is everywhere, a fragile yet strong presence, a vulnerable child, unarmed and unprotected, a future that is always being reborn. Hope!

"Hope makes me go on living," some people say when they are near to death. Others echo Charles Péguy: "The faith that I choose is hope!" But it is a hope that is quite different from resignation.

The journey that we make during Advent—which means, of course, approach or coming—is a patient descent into the depths to discover the hidden seed that has already yielded so much fruit in the soil of men and women. From the ruins of Jerusalem to the birth in humility in Bethlehem, from exile in the desert to baptism in the desert—everything spurs us on to go further.

There are three stages on this journey: the season of the future, the time when Isaiah expresses the appeal made by the God who never forgets, the time of the forerunner, when the prophet calls us out into the desert to show us the Bridegroom, the God of the covenant, and the time of giving birth, when the Spirit encloses the virgin and the barren woman so that the source that we have hoped for and have been promised will flow. Advent begins with oracular pronouncements of a political restoration and ends with our gazing at a king who is gentle and humble in heart. Between this beginning and this end, however, we have followed John, the sign that "God is gracious."

Isaiah, exile and restoration! Living today in a state of continuous crisis, we express ourselves almost unthinkingly in the language of prophecy. We say, for example: We must prepare the way for a new world, there is a future for us, it is possible, we must face that future—let us accept it! The prophets of the Old Testament were deeply committed politically. They may even be the only men who have ever been able to avoid despair in speaking politically, because they were speaking about the world as God wanted it to be. Our Advent would be a useless and empty prayer if we were to read Isaiah's words and hold ourselves aloof from the misery, injustice and torture that cause such pain in the world today. Hope is only worthy of faith if it embraces the cry of those who suffer.

In Advent we celebrate the hope of a whole people. Liturgy is, after all, never an individual activity. In that celebration, however, we may, like our fathers exiled on the banks of the rivers of Babylon, "sit down and weep" (see Ps 137:1). In the past, we were firmly established in the city, but now we are no more than a remnant. But it is for that "remnant" that the prophet proclaims the good news. Hope would no longer exist if it were based on the strength of those in power! The call of the desert does not consist of empty poetic sounds made to attract tourists in a hurry!

The way in the Bible becomes narrower and narrower the more closely it approaches its end, Jesus. This is because Jesus comes closest to the poor outside the city walls, in the heart of the desert. John the Baptist has a vitally important place there. He was sent by God to proclaim the need for conversion and to point to the true Messiah, without having any place of his own. He was above all humble, since that is what hope always has to be.

John's ambition in the desert was to reconstitute the people of God. A community was reborn—a Church stripped of the polish of the Pharisees and the solemnities of the priesthood, a Church waiting impatiently for the coming. The old covenant ended on an extraordinary note: "Our God is coming!" This is one aspect of the prophet John, of course, but there is also that other fragile aspect which we identify with his and our question: "Are you the one who is to come?" (Mt 11:3; Lk 7:19). What a dramatic question that is! It reflects his fear to commit himself to the cause of a Messiah who is apparently too gentle and vulnerable to overthrow the adversary. All the same, for us John is still the one who points to the Lamb of God. The icons of the Eastern Church show him holding out both hands to receive the joy of the Bridegroom.

He is coming! Our journey continues and our destination gradually becomes focused on humble dwellings, pregnant women and displaced persons. The Spirit can blow like a tornado, but now becomes a gentle morning breeze. The Magnificat may well be a revolutionary song and the Visitation may be a wild dance recalling the recovery of the ark, but the fact remains that these two women, Mary and Elizabeth, sing and dance with great joy for the children that they have conceived.

Hope, then, is a little girl whose hand we have to hold, but who is really leading us. Advent will end when Christmas comes. We will go then to the place where the shepherds are. Happy are those who believe in that birth! It is believing in a future that is always possible. Isaiah had prophesied: "The maiden is with child and will soon give birth to a son" (Is 7:14), and it is the task of prophets to speak without knowing. The name of Immanuel sings in us like crazy hope. God is with us and he has the face of a child. Children are the only ones who really know what God wants.

"Righteousness and peace now embrace" (Ps 85:11) and "the wolf lives with the lamb" (Is 11:6). It sounds like a children's game. But what is hope but living at the level of impossibility, as though we were playing? Does not God tell us to build up the world without any instruction manual but our own imagination? So we should never attempt to stop children playing.

FROM THE MONDAY OF THE FIRST WEEK TO THE WEDNESDAY OF THE SECOND WEEK: THE SEASON OF THE FUTURE

ISAIAH, THE PROPHET OF ADVENT
Isaiah is the best known of all the prophets and certainly the one most frequently quoted in the gospels. But the name "Isaiah" covers several authors, and the sixty-six chapters of the book are the result of literary activity covering many centuries.

Chapters 1 to 39 have been attributed to the prophet himself, but they do not all come from the same hand. The author began to preach about 740 B.C., at the end of the reign of King Uzziah, David's eleventh successor on the throne of Jerusalem. He gives an account of his calling which sets out all that is essential in his message. He had an experience of the transcendence of God in the temple and God was for him the "Holy One of Israel"—a jealous God who would not share and a hidden God who wanted man to work with him in shaping history. The prophet expected his fellow Israelites to believe so firmly that they would if necessary disregard human reason. He was a man of God who was deeply immersed in the politics of his people, and his ministry was carried out during a particularly troubled period of Israel's history. Solomon's kingdom had not lasted very long and had soon split into two—the northern kingdom of Israel and the southern kingdom of Judah. Weakened by internal dissensions, Solomon's successors had also had to confront a powerful enemy outside—Assyria. In 732, Samaria fell after repeated attacks by Tiglath-pileser III.

It was at this time that King Ahaz asked his Assyrian neighbor to protect his country. It was, then, when the king was ready to abandon the independence of the country that the prophet announced the birth of Immanuel, who was possibly the prince, Hezekiah. Isaiah was in a very real sense the conscience of the nation and he could not agree to his sovereign endangering the sovereignty of the elected dynasty. Later on, he also opposed Hezekiah, when the latter wanted to enter into an alliance with Egypt against Assyria. In every case of political opportunism, the prophet always stressed the demand made by faithfulness to God. In this case, he was convinced that the Assyrian invasion was God's will—the people had to be punished for their sins. But Jerusalem had to remain the center of the world and the only legitimate throne. Two themes which Isaiah's disciples continued to emphasize were messianism and the universal function of the holy city.

Jerusalem fell in 587, overthrown by Babylon, and the noble population followed the last king of Judah into exile. Then, with the fickleness of fortune, proud Babylon had in turn to capitulate to the power of Persia. Some of the Jews believed that these events were the result of intervention by the Persian god Marduk. This led an anonymous prophet—the one we call Second Isaiah—to remind the people sharply that Yahweh was the only Lord of the world and its history (chapters 40-55). He also proclaimed the end of the exile and the return to Israel. In 538, Cyrus' decree put an end to the deportation of the people.

The prophet described the return of the exiles as an exodus that was even more wonderful than that led by Moses. The mountains of Sinai were replaced by a way of triumph, worthy of a king's retinue. Yahweh, who had left Jerusalem to join his people in exile (Ez 10:18-22), also followed this royal highway to return to his city. The first group of people reached Jerusalem in 537. They were the elite of the nation and their task was to raise up the survivors of Israel and carry the light of God to foreigners.

But the apotheosis that had been proclaimed was still a long way off. The returned exiles encountered hostility on the part of those who had stayed behind. Jerusalem remained an ambivalent place with a suspicious population and the rebuilding of the temple took far too long. This collapse of the nation's hopes led the prophets to attempt to rescue what Second Isaiah had done by adapting his teaching to the changed circumstances (chapters 56-66, known as the work of Third Isaiah). The heart of their message can be found in chapters 60 to 62, which announce the glorious resurrection of Jerusalem.

Several prophets, then, were known by one name. "Isaiah" is in itself a symbol. Some of the oracles proved to be wrong, since events turned out differently. The disciples did not hesitate to reinstate the preaching of the first prophet. In spite or because of this, the prophetic message as a whole gives an impression of solidity and continuity. The Israelites saw that prophecy less as preaching than as a promise "that remained relevant for their own time for as long as it was not completely fulfilled." This extension of the idea of prophecy was made possible by the faith of the Israelites, who believed above all in God's faithfulness and for whom God's guarantee lasted beyond all the vicissitudes of history. As Isaiah himself said: "The grass withers, the flower fades, but the word of our God remains for ever" (40:8).

■

God, you console your people,
  Lord, have mercy.

Shepherd, you raise up the weak,
  Christ, have mercy.

Jesus, you are gentle and humble in heart,
  Lord, have mercy.

We thank you, God our Father,
  and praise you for your wonderful acts.
You fill in the great ravines
  that exist between men.
You show us the way
  through our labyrinths and dead-ends.
You lead the exile back home.

Like the sun rising faithfully at daybreak,
  you let man be reborn every day.
  He is wretched, but you cover him in glory
  and place on his forehead
  the diadem of the children of God.
The whole of the universe, Lord,
  is full of joy and cheerful
  in its praise and thanksgiving,
  which is for you.

When you come to us, Lord,
  love and truth meet
  and justice and peace embrace.
Join our hands together, Lord,
  so that we may all build

*the city where all men are one
in the unity of love.*

*The one whom you have given us in your grace
is already in the midst of us.*
*Lord our God,
you have placed in our hands
the body of your Son, handed over for the world.*
*We ask you:
may his presence among us be our light
and may we go unhesitatingly
to the place where we shall encounter your love.*

MONDAY OF THE FIRST WEEK

AT THE HEART OF THE WORLD
Is 4:2–6 (Year A): After the rain—fine weather! The prophet describes a future that is rich in promises. At the beginning of his prophetic mission, the kingdom of Judah was enjoying great prosperity. But this led to all kinds of injustices, and these the prophet denounced.

The people's behavior was so bad that they richly deserved the misfortunes that struck them. Yet the prophet never ceased to believe that a "remnant" of believers would survive. On "that day" (verse 2) Jerusalem would be adorned with glory. The faithful remnant would not receive ornaments and costly garments (see 3:16–17) but divine favors, and would be not only the "branch of Yahweh" but also the "fruit of the earth."

First, Yahweh would purify Jerusalem and the surrounding country with fire and wind, like a winnower separating the seed from the chaff. Then he would once again "come and rest" on the city, covering it with his shadow. The wonders of the exodus would be renewed and a covenant, like the one made on Sinai, would be concluded under the wedding canopy.

Is 2:1–5 (Years B and C): Jerusalem, the holy city—countless pilgrims had come there to learn from the priests how to praise God and to "walk in his paths" and had trodden the stones of its streets, reddened with the blood of sacrifices.

Jerusalem is the foundation of peace. We have to interpret the meaning of the great movements of the people there in the light of Revelation—they go again and again to the town where they "will not need lamplight or sunlight, because the Lord God will be shining on them" (Rv 22:5). Every nation will accept the judgment of God and his reign will be universal. Ps 122 was sung by the pilgrims when they were leaving Jerusalem. They recalled the good days spent in the city and asked God to grant it peace.

Mt 8:5–11: A new heaven and a new earth—the time of the fulfillment has arrived! A Roman centurion comes to Jesus and asks him to heal his servant. It is a delicate situation and Jesus cures the man at a distance, in this way not making himself unclean by touching a non-Jew. But the Roman soldier is also a man of great depth. He is himself subject to higher authority and therefore senses that Jesus' words may come from elsewhere. Jesus does not conceal his admiration for the man. The true sons of Abraham are those who believe him, and they will inherit the kingdom.

■

Come, divine Messiah! Advent, which we begin now, is a cry, a prayer, a time of waiting and expectation. Yet there are many messiahs today. Must we wait for someone else (see Mt 11:3; Lk 7:19)—someone who will succeed where so many of our hopes have been disappointed? There are so many different kinds of messianism—political, social and economic as well as religious— and they are offered to us as powerful and attractive and as the cure for our wasting away and depression. They also call for unconditional obedience on the part of their followers. Yet one after another they all collapse in the end, crushed by their own totalitarian spirit, just as Jerusalem, that proud city, also succumbed under the weight of its own haughty bearing at the very place where the priests saw the nations and the "peoples without number" arriving.

But Christian messianism is different from this. It is not founded on human strength. It is rooted in the words of the prophets and they never ceased to say: "Be converted! Turn back to God!" Our Messiah is a Messiah of peace and of the poor. He is a Messiah for those who

have experienced the emptiness of pride and self-sufficiency, a Messiah who has trodden our paths and who has come to save the one who is lost. "Lord, I am not worthy to have you under my roof; just give the word . . ."

There is always a utopian element in messianism. But whether or not that utopia becomes a reality depends on us. Will we ever be humble enough to regard ourselves as poor, without rights and powerless? If we can do that, then "that day" it will happen that "nation will not lift sword against nation and there will be no more training for war."

■

Yes, we thank you,
God our justice, hope of the world.
You created man
  so that he would share with his brothers
  love, peace and happiness.
And when he turns away from you,
  a prisoner of life's anxieties,
  you give him your Son,
  handed over for freeing of captives.
That is why we lift up our heads
  as dawn is rising on the horizon
  and sing together with the saints
  "Come, Lord Jesus!"
  and acclaim his presence among us.

You came to bring peace into men's hearts—
  Lord, be with us!

You care for the poor and the oppressed—
  Christ, stay with us!
The Spirit of power rests on you—
  Lord, change us!

God, Father of life,
  may your name be blessed.
God of our joyful cries
  and God of our tears,
  may you be blessed.

You did not make man
  to enclose him in death.
You come to meet us
  and life goes ahead of you, singing,
God of the promise,
  God of hope,
  we bless you.
You know where our halting steps are taking us
  and do not forsake us
  when our hopes are disappointed.
You make your light shine on us
  and you console us.
We thank you, Lord.
Yes, we can even now climb the hills
  and proclaim your good news,
  singing.

TUESDAY OF THE FIRST WEEK

CRAZY HOPE
Is 11:1–10: King Ahaz went ahead with his plan to strengthen Jerusalem's defenses, even though Isaiah had suggested that he ought to put his trust in the fragile sign of the Immanuel. But the king and his counselors turned a deaf ear to this advice and the prophet therefore ceased to speak for a while.

Should that Immanuel be identified with the prince, Hezekiah? Even now critics are very divided about this. What is certain is that Isaiah proclaimed at a particularly dark time in the nation's history that God was with his people.

The prophet comes back again and again to this theme which was very close to his heart. He even borrowed certain features from the language of the scribes which enabled him to paint a lifelike portrait of the expected hero. He describes the Immanuel as a man of character and understanding who, in his concern to carry out his sacred duty to God and the people, will restore the ancient monarchic ideal of justice and integrity. His reign will bring back the golden age of paradise on earth when animals lived at peace with each other and with man. Even that ancient enemy of man, the snake, was to be quite harmless.

Ps 72 is a description of the ideal king. He behaves as a father toward his subjects and guarantees their prosperity and well-being. Lk 10:21–24: The prophets' knowledge of the messianic age was, as it were, veiled. The mystery was to be revealed to the "little ones." Jesus gives thanks to the Father because the "poor of Yahweh" are the only ones who read the signs and have access to God. His blessing is reminiscent of that in Dn 2:20–23. Like the Chaldaean diviners, the Pharisees and scribes were, for all their knowledge, incapable of interpreting the signs of the coming of the kingdom.

A crazy hope seizes hold of us. The days of justice and peace are coming. But where are those days? What change will there be this Advent? "Happy the eyes that see what you see." But what do we see?

Hope is like this—if it was not crazy, it would no longer be hope. Wise men, scholars and political leaders have no need of it. But a ray of sunlight, a comforting word or an outstretched hand are worth more than a thousand peace treaties to the little ones, the poor. They know how to interpret the invisible signs because they are used to living at the level of what cannot be perceived. It could perhaps be said that they believed very meekly, but, with Jesus, they are in good company.

Have you ever seen a tree that was obviously ahead of its time and budding too early in the year? As soon as a frost comes, those buds are killed and there is no fruit in the autumn. That is true, of course, but the tree's boldness is the sign of a spring that will still come, despite the winter. We all need hope, even if it is crazy.

"A shoot springs from the stock of Jesse . . ." He will set the poor and the wretched free. Jesus came—without a crown, without any weapons, as a servant. He still comes today—into the hearts of the little ones waiting for him. Will the wolf live with the lamb? Will man live with man?

Why not? It depends on you—on whether you welcome the Spirit of God. Jesus is already lifted up on the cross, like a standard for the nations to see. Happy is the man who follows in his footsteps. He can give body to his hope. For that hope is a delicate shoot from a trunk stripped bare. It is the dawn of renewal in a night that cannot last forever.

■

Who will treat the oppressed with justice?
Who will decide with integrity for the abandoned people?
Lord, you are tenderness and you are gentle
   and in your heart you understand the suffering of the humble.
Do not forget your love for us
and raise up those who stumble on the way,
   for you are our Savior
   forever and ever.

WEDNESDAY OF THE FIRST WEEK

THE BANQUET OF THE POOR
Is 25:6–10a: Chapter 25 is part of what is usually known as the "Apocalypse" of Isaiah (chapters 24–27). Narrative alternates with lyrical elements in this group of chapters. Chapter 24 describes the confrontation between the forces of evil and the forces of good and it ends by proclaiming the victory of God, who "will be king on Mount Zion in Jerusalem" (24:23).

There he "will prepare a banquet for all peoples" at which the richest dishes, usually reserved for the deity, will be served. It is in fact a festive meal of the kind usually taken in the company of Yahweh himself, during communion sacrifices. Even the veil covering the eyes of the pagans will be torn and they too will be able to see God's face. This is an ancient biblical symbol, according to which food and drink lead to the beatific vision. What, then, can man do, confronted with this promise? It is only natural for him to thank God. Hope is followed by rejoicing. Ps 23 was originally a psalm of trust in God, but the Church made it a song of entry into the promised land—the "meadows of green grass." The images of wine, corn and oil also turn our minds toward the Eucharist.

Mt 15:29–37: The kingdom has come. Jesus takes all man's weaknesses and illnesses on himself. Sins are wiped out and the messianic table is set for all men. There is only one condition required from those who want to take their place there—they must believe in Jesus Christ. In the text preceding this passage, the faith of the Canaanite woman obtained healing for her daughter.

Jesus presides at the table of the kingdom. Just as Yahweh fed his people in the desert, so Jesus gives us his "flesh" to eat today. Here he takes loaves, gives thanks and shares them. The whole of Passover-Easter is present in this story of the loaves—the desert Passover for the twelve tribes of Israel and the Easter of history which brings all men together.

■

"Everything is ready. Come to the wedding feast" (Mt 22:4). When God comes, it will be to fill the hungry with good things and to give life in abundance to those who long for it—the lame, the blind, the crippled and the poor. It is above all for them that Jesus takes the seven loaves and multiplies them infinitely, satisfying their hunger and going beyond his own prodigality. It is for them that God prepares a banquet of the most festive kind.

Do you ever think of God and the most tasty food and the most heady wine at the same time? Do you think of God and at the same time long to live at the deepest level with the whole of your being? Well, God and the fullness of life are the same thing.

God comes for the poor. We often say that, but do we really accept our own poverty? Not so much the poverty of sinners as that more radical poverty of the crippled beings that we are, wounded by a life which we long with all our being to have, but which has only ever been given to us in part? A poverty that envelops us like a mourning veil? Once we begin to accept that poverty, we shall begin to call out to God, since God comes to change our mourning into a dance and our desert into a table of grace. How shall we ever meet God if we do not learn how to call out to life, like a blind person calling out to the sun?

Longing, hoping and then exulting and being in communion—those are the words of poverty. It was for the poor that Jesus set the table. "If any man is hungry, let him come to me" (cf. Jn 7:37). "Long life to your hearts, all you who seek God" (Ps 69:32). On our road through the desert, each Eucharist is a table of hope and a feast of the poor. Happy are those who are invited. Happy is the man who opens his hands in his great longing to live. Happy are those who are crying when the Lord comes to wipe away the tears from their faces. That is his gesture of tenderness. That is his gesture when he takes bread to place his body handed over in our hands. "Come, Lord Jesus!" (Rv 22:20).

■

We thank you, God our hope,
  through Jesus Christ, your beloved Son,
  who came to gather together
  those who had gone off aimlessly
  into the desert of renunciation.
Your are blessed, God.
  You satisfy man's longings.
  You make life rise up
  stronger than death
  and more gentle than tears.
At this festive table,
  where the banquet of your kingdom
  is already celebrated,
  and with all those
  who place their hope in you,
  God, Father of the poor, we bless you.

THURSDAY OF THE FIRST WEEK

AN IMPREGNABLE CITY
Is 26:1–6: It is better to take refuge in the Lord than to rely on men (see Ps 118:8). The pagans have put their confidence in the thickness of the walls of their citadel, but now their place of refuge is like "straw trodden in the dung pit" (Is 25:10).

The point of departure for the "Apocalypse" of Isaiah seems to have been the laying waste of the land of the Moabites. How Israel must have rejoiced to see her ancient enemy defeated. When they learned of this disaster, the people of Jerusalem congratulated themselves on their good fortune to be living in a city with natural fortifications and a double rampart. But above all it was Yahweh who was the "everlasting rock." He guarded their city and they put their trust in him. Rejoice, Jerusalem, for the impregnable city has been overturned, but you can open your gates.

The memory of a ceremony of thanksgiving in the temple is preserved in Ps 118. The gates open to admit the pilgrim, surrounded by his family and friends, and the priests ministering in the temple congratulate him for having chosen to trust in the strength of Yahweh rather than that of the princes of this world.

Mt 7:21, 24–27: Jesus is coming to the end of his teaching on the mountain. His last words are a warning not to reduce what he has said simply to the level of an object to be discussed or analyzed. His is the word of life, and man should let it bear fruit in him.

Then there is the little fable in praise of the man with foresight who builds his home on certain values, composed of such familiar elements as the bare rock, the sand and the rushing stream flooding the dry wadi. But what value could be more certain than the person of Jesus? In Ps 118:22, he is called the "keystone."

■

"We have a strong city." Who can overthrow us? We own half the world. Who is equal to us? A long litany of human pride, full of self-confident boasting and a refrain echoing wars, the cry of the exploited and the death of the oppressed. An unexpected devaluation of the gold standard and all the inhabitants of citadels built on shifting sand are also shaking on their foundations. Is not history itself written on the basis of civilizations that have collapsed?

But man is incorrigible and there is a great gulf between human history and history as seen from the perspective of God, in that astonishing kingdom where the poor are given the honorable places and the humble are filled with joy. "There is no eternal city for us in this life, but we look for one in the life to come" (Heb 13:14). Are we building for a hundred years or forever? Is our Jerusalem one that boasts of its rampart and outer wall or is it one that will "come down from God out of heaven, as beautiful as a bride all dressed for her husband" (Rv 21:2)? Is it a city protected against attack in war or a place that is vulnerable to love? A city of men or a city of God? As another psalm says, the man who seeks refuge in the Lord is like Mount Zion. Yet Zion was also razed to the ground. The man who puts his trust in the Lord will never be lost.

What, then, is your faith, man—what do you trust? Money? Power? Security? If you do, you will certainly fall, like the house built on sand. There is only one certain value and that is called God.

■

You build peace firmly, Lord,
for those who trust in you.

We pray to you
for those responsible for peace in the world:
  may they build the future on the rock of justice;
for those who possess the good things of this world:
  that they may open the doors of well-being to all men;
for Christians who call on your name:
  that they may move from faith to acts of love
  and solidarity with the poor.

FRIDAY OF THE FIRST WEEK

THE DEATH OF THE TYRANTS
Is 29:17–24: Look at the country that the Lord has given to your fathers. Everywhere there is injustice and oppression, the administration is corrupt and the poor people have no means of complaining against their rulers. The iniquity of the judgments made by the king's tribunals is in fact a "tyrant," and those who constitute that "tyrant" are the royal counselors and men in secure positions. The word of God is no longer heard. Flatterers are in favor. Is that situation really just and holy?

But God will overthrow those who mock him in this way. There will be a fundamental change. Lebanon will become like Carmel and the proud forest will be no more than an orchard. Then the blind will see and the deaf will hear. The poor will exult in the Lord. The Lord will be faithful to his promises and blot out the shame of the house of Jacob.

Ps 27 may be the trusting prayer of a man accused of homicide who has sought refuge in the temple and is protesting that he is innocent. The psalm is his appeal made to God.

Mt 9:27–31: Two blind men on the road. In Matthew, they follow the lepers, the centurion's son, Peter's mother-in-law, the demoniacs, the paralyzed man, the woman with a hemorrhage and Jairus' daughter—a whole series of miraculous healings. But surely the kingdom of God is like that. God comes to man and takes his sickness and his sin on himself.

These two blind men see again and men are able to hold up their heads once more. Death is overcome and the tyranny that it has been able to exert over mankind is conquered. Whenever men and women recognize Jesus Christ as the Son of David, a community is born to the life of grace.

■

How easy it is to have the poor people condemned—those who do not even know what their rights are. Just throw a little powder in their eyes and they are blinded and given over into the hands of those who are trying to make them, innocent people, fall. However often the book of the law is read in their presence, it remains a dead letter. Who will give them the key to enable them to find themselves in the law? From one generation to the next, tyrants mock God and man in this way. Sometimes tyranny is monstrous in size and quite open, humiliating whole nations. At other times, it may be insidious and on a small scale, causing individuals to stumble. Tell your lies. Some truth will always remain.

"In a short time, a very short time," the prophet says, "all that will change." But the poor wonder when it will change. In the meantime, their darkness continues and will not be lightened until someone comes their way and asks them quite simply: "Do you believe that I can do that for you?"

Then Jesus will open the eyes of the blind and it will be the end of tyranny. How will that come about? Jesus tells every man that there

is dignity in being called "man" and that it is enough for him to hold up his head in the presence of his oppressor for the tyranny to be overcome, because, if tyranny fails to degrade man, it has failed in its aim. Jesus Christ tells the world that God loves man and a glimmer of love is enough to overthrow the evil power of tyranny.

"In a short time, a very short time," the Lord says. So let your heart be made open by God and you will see that your poverty is really a source of happiness. But do not tell everyone about it. Who would believe you? For centuries tyrants have thought that they ruled the world. Poor blind men! With their eyes wide open, they have seen nothing but darkness. But the day has dawned for us—the day of inner light.

∎

God, you stand up for the poor
   and we ask you:
open our eyes to men's misery
and change our hearts,
   so that we may bear witness to your justice
   and work for a new world
   where your light will shine forever.

SATURDAY OF THE FIRST WEEK

THE STARS, THE SUN AND GOOD NEWS

Is 30:19–21, 23–26: The people have rebelled against God. The Israelites have once again been disobedient sons, rejecting the law. They are even asking the prophets to proclaim only good, favorable oracles. It will, then, not be long before they are punished and Israel's stiff neck is broken (see 30:14).

Yet Isaiah still declares that they will be reconciled with Yahweh. As soon as he sees the first signs of repentance, he will be gracious and pardon them. He will give them bread and water in their distress and the voice of the prophets will be heard again. There will be abundant rain, the earth will be fertile and their beasts will prosper. These will be signs of God's good will. "Salted fodder" was, of course, something that was eaten with particular relish by domestic animals. According to an Arab proverb, fresh fodder is the bread of camels, but salted fodder is their jam.

The concluding verses of this passage have apocalyptic overtones. When the proud walls fall, watercourses will make the hills fertile and the moon and the sun will shine with unparalleled strength. Ps 147 is a hymn celebrating God's great mercy. The Lord heals broken hearts and binds up wounds.

Mt 9:35—10:1, 6–8: The crowds are "distressed and prostrate" like "sheep without a shepherd." Men, abandoned by their rightful masters and wandering about—this is a common scene in the Old Testament. It is to such men that Jesus comes to proclaim God's plan. His unique authority is revealed in all that he says and does. Here he gives that authority to a group of twelve disciples, who represent all those who recognize in Christ the fulfillment of God's promise. Their ministry is based on that of their Master and it leads to judgment—healings and exorcisms are the signs of victory over evil.

We should note that before he handed over his authority to the Twelve, Jesus prayed to the Father. This shows that the Christian mission is not simply a human task—it is the Spirit that gives it life. The disciples are not confirmed in their apostolic task because of any merit of their own. They have "received without pay" and they should "give without pay."

∎

According to Ps 147, "the Lord decides the number of the stars" and "heals broken hearts." It is not simply in the twentieth century that men have believed that there is a relationship between astrology and consoling the afflicted. In biblical times too, there were countless astrologers overshadowing the work of the God who made the sun shine "seven times brighter on that day." What, then, is the relationship between the good news of God and all the inventors of good news to whom so many brokenhearted people run? Is the Bible itself—and especially its apocalyptic passages—no more than an additional mystification? Is the "mystery" of God himself something that is seen in an astrologer's crystal ball?

These are serious questions. Whatever the gospel may say, the sick are not always (radically) cured and the dead do not rise again now any more or less than they did in the past. If leprosy is less common now—and to be honest it is only a little less common—that is largely thanks to human care and advances in medical science. We really long to be spared all those (falsely) spiritual interpretations of the gospel that do not measure up to the physical suffering of so many men and women. The human body is not a useless article and the promise of heavenly consolation later—always later—does not satisfy my hunger or dry my tears—even in the name of the Bible.

Jesus and his disciples undoubtedly cured the sick, but they did it according to the conviction that prevailed at that time, that the body and the soul belonged inseparably to each other. This idea is always recurring in the Bible. We should not, however, lose ourselves in neurotic mystifications, but recognize that we are living in an authentically evangelical tradition if we embrace all the positive achievements of modern medicine and scientific research and at the same time care tenderly for our fellow men. The sun shining ceaselessly—that is an image. God drying the tears of those who weep—that is reality. The two are interrelated.

We should be stopping places on the journey of the God who feels deeply for men in their suffering and abandonment. Advent ought to be the season when he calls together all those who are longing for a new world and are realistically committed to working for it. They may, after all, be the only ones who are genuinely living out God's poetic experience.

Have you ever tried to count the stars in heaven around a camp fire? Have you ever reflected how many there are on earth? God calls each star by its name. He calls each one of us by name—because each one is a star and he wants to see it shine in the night. Do we shine in that way?

MONDAY OF THE SECOND WEEK

THE WASTELAND WILL BLOOM
Is 35:1–10: Chapters 34 and 35, which were composed later than the rest of the Book of Isaiah, are known as the "little Apocalypse." They originated with the same event, and while Chapter 34 describes the fall of the Edomites, Chapter 35 expresses the relief felt by the Jews after the defeat of their enemies.

Gradually, however, this passage came to be seen less as a song celebrating a military victory than as a hymn anticipating Yahweh's coming among his people. On that day, the whole of nature will rejoice together with Jerusalem. Water will flow and make the desert fertile, and dry grass will be replaced by the reeds and papyrus of the marshland. Through this smiling countryside will run a sacred way that is closed to the ungodly and to wild animals. The wonder of that road will be that those who follow it will not be afraid, but will go forward with firm footsteps. God will have visited his people.

Verses 10–13 of Ps 85 are Yahweh's reply to the prayer of his people asking him for life and happiness. These words proclaim a new era when God will come and live in the country.

Lk 5:17–26: Jesus and Simon Peter are face to face. Jesus does now what God had so often done in the past for his people—he offers his disciple a word of forgiveness and blessing. "Leave me, Lord," Peter says. "I am a sinful man." Jesus' reply is: "Do not be afraid; from now on it is men you will catch."

It is, then, an offer of reconciliation. Israel had again and again gone astray on the paths of idolatry and injustice. At the same time, the people had always been aware of their treachery and had never doubted that their God would be faithful. They had continued to rely on his grace. They knew that he would free them from their obsessions, just as he had delivered their ancestors from slavery in Egypt. So, when Jesus strengthened the knees of the paralyzed man, he was giving Israel a sign. He was causing the source of the disorder that was undermining the whole of creation to dry up and bringing the people back to their covenant with God.

■

"We have seen the flowers of tenderness bloom in our deserts—we have seen a new peace dawn in our world." When children hear these lines, which are, of course, rooted in the Old Testament, and are asked: "Where shall we see that happen?" they often say they have seen it in good people in whom "righteousness and peace embrace." Will children be the last survivors in the kingdom?

We should begin by knowing the desert. From the Sahel to the northeast and from our shanty towns to the psychiatric wards, the earth is barren, people go crazy in the desert, their knees give way and death rules. Why, then, is the desert the special place of encounter with God? Surely it is because God always comes as a source of life and renewal. Man has again and again to accept that he needs to be saved and that his sinfulness has even today reduced the world to a desert of fierce, cruel conflict.

"Say to all faint hearts, 'Courage! Do not be afraid.'" Jesus sees a wretched paralytic, looks at him tenderly and imprints boundless happiness on his features. The healed man leaps up and glorifies God. The Son of Man appears and opens a sacred way through our dried up land. His face is a source of joy for the poor he loves. Do you believe that the wasteland will bloom when man looks at his fellow man with love? Will righteousness and peace at last embrace and make the poor joyful?

■

Our hands have worked, but in vain;
　our knees are weak
　and our strength is exhausted.
Humiliated, we have cried to you
　and you have heard us.
Speak again in our hearts, Lord,
　and strengthen us in our weakness.
You give life to our barren earth.

TUESDAY OF THE SECOND WEEK

THE GOD OF TENDERNESS
Is 40:1–11: The first verses of Chapter 40 form a prologue of several voices that sets the tone for the whole of the work of Second Isaiah, which is often called the "Book of the Consolation of Israel." From 587 B.C. onward, Jerusalem had been bitterly lamenting its sinfulness, but now its sin had been expiated and messengers were proclaiming the end of its exile. Not only Israel but also the other nations were going to witness an exodus that was even more wonderful than the first. Yahweh was going ahead of the Babylonian exiles on a way recently marked out through the Syrian desert and Jerusalem would soon be able to announce to the towns of Judah: "Here is your God."

The prophet is saying that God is faithful, that he never forgets his people and that he will meet them in the desert. Later Judaism interpreted the prophet's words as an invitation to withdraw before the final restoration of Israel. But on God's highway, the forerunner takes on a human form. In the first place, he would seem to be the prophet Elijah going ahead of God and then, later, John the Baptist preceding God made man. Ps 95 is similar to a hymn and sings of the lordship of Yahweh. Not only believers are invited to place their offerings before the King's throne—the whole of the created world is celebrating a feast, for the Lord is coming "to judge the world with justice."

Mt 18:12–14: "He is like a shepherd feeding his flock" (Is 40:11)—how many times the image of the shepherd is used in the Bible! It goes back to the person of Jacob walking with his sheep. The prophet Ezekiel used it to point out the defects of Israel's leaders and their failure to govern the people, whom they should have served (Ez 34). The same prophet also announced that God himself would go ahead of the flock and look for the lost sheep in the holy places where the pagans worshiped.

Jesus is quite unlike the Pharisees, enshrouded in their own righteousness. He proclaims the joy of a God who prefers the conversion of a sinner to the self-satisfaction of the righteous whose lives are in a rut. In the tradition of Ezekiel, he calls on the disciples to do everything possible to bring their straying brothers back. For Matthew, each Christian has a unique place in the Church, which is not just an anonymous collectivity. Each Christian has the task of sharing in the Father's concern for sinners.

■

"Console my people," says God. Yes, he consoles his people. Have you reflected about the tenderness of God? He does not want one of his little ones to be lost. Like a shepherd, he leads his flock. The Bible again and again attempts to express the inexpressible—the gentleness of God that is so wonderfully united to his power. The God who comes subduing all things with his victorious arm is also the shepherd who carries his lambs in his arm and takes care of his ewes.

At that time, when exile in Babylon had made Israel lose heart almost completely, God had to console his people and to lead the great procession that was to cross the desert and return to the homeland. There were enormous difficulties ahead: ravines to be filled in, mountains to be laid low, ridges to be crossed and twisting paths to be made straight. But God promised and his words were to be trusted: he would lead the caravan and go at its pace.

Is it so very different now? There are still so many walls to break down and so many obstacles to overcome if the people of God are to live in peace with each other in a world at peace, united in brotherhood—a world in which the little ones are loved the most and human beings respond to each other with their hearts rather than with weapons. Sometimes the task appears impossible and we seem to be living in exile, far from a Gospel that has lost its flavor of good news.

"Console my people," says God. "Shout with a loud voice, joyful messenger!" It is above all the tenderness of God, his love, patience and gentleness that we have to rediscover. We have to let ourselves be carried in his arms. We have to let ourselves be the wounded ones in a world gone astray. For God is coming and he will change our earth. Happy are those who will welcome him with open hearts. They will, with God himself, be called to work for a new kind of peace.

■

Yes, Father, we give you thanks.
  We shout aloud with joy

and sing: You have worked wonders for us.
You fill in the ravines separating man from man,
  you mark out a way through the maze of our loneliness
  and you give the exile your hand
  and lead him home.
That is why
  the whole universe is full of a new song
  and our voices echo in response to it.

WEDNESDAY OF THE SECOND WEEK

A LIGHT BURDEN

Is 40:25–31: Israel in exile often gives the impression of having completely lost heart. The people are always saying they have no future and there is no salvation for them. They dispute everything, call everything into question and accuse God of having forgotten them.

So the prophet, unable to endure these criticisms any longer, speaks out. He knows that Israel's faith must be based on a strong sense of God's faithfulness. He tells the people to look a little further and see God as unique, incomparable and holy, as the one who has no accounts to render to anyone and who never ceases to carry out his work of salvation. He is Lord over the whole world. Why, then, should the Israelites do what the Babylonians do and worship the stars, seeking horoscopes from them?

Ps 103 is hymnic in form and blesses the Lord for the favors that he is always bestowing on those who trust in him.

Mt 11:28–30: "He gives strength to the wearied, he strengthens the powerless." Echoing the prophet Isaiah, Jesus invites men to learn from him. Isaiah spoke to the exiled Israelites—Jesus speaks to all who are separated from God. The scribes made the law almost too heavy to bear and set ordinary people, who were unable to find their way through it, at a distance. But Jesus goes to the heart of the matter and relieves the little ones of such useless restraints. His commandment is simple and so his burden is light.

∎

Surely all of us dream sometimes of a simple way of life that is free of all the countless restraints that make every day sad from the moment we wake up. And those that cast the darkest shadow perhaps are the religious restraints: Don't do this! Be on your guard against that! Thou shalt not . . . They seem to be laws devised by churchmen constantly on the lookout for terrible aberrations. They also have an unpleasant taste of sadism that is quite alien to the Gospel.

It is not that Jesus wants us to be easy-going. He knows better than anyone that man's heart has to be put right again and again. But only he knows how it can be put right—his yoke is easy, however essential it may be. Christians have to bear a burden, but, compared with the burdens imposed on them by other men, it is liberating. Those who have taken the yoke of love onto themselves will understand that.

Nothing is more difficult to believe than an image of God the Creator constantly turning over a new law to impose on men in his mind. Perhaps we should say: against men! Is not life itself heavy enough for most of us to carry? It is true that the infinite God is infinitely interested in that microcosm, man, but his way of behaving toward man is diametrically opposed to that of the gods invented by those in power. Our God is "gentle and humble in heart."

So, when you feel that you cannot continue as a Christian and religion seems to be overburdened with the weight of the law, think about God and breathe again: God is gentle, God is humble, the Lord of life is humble.

∎

To all those who are crushed by the weight of their misery,
  come, Jesus, gentle and humble in heart,

To all those who are disheartened by the burden of the law,
  come, Messiah of the little and simple ones.

To all those at a distance from God because of weariness or resentment,
  come, Jesus, image of the Father.

FROM THE THURSDAY OF THE SECOND WEEK
TO THE FRIDAY OF THE THIRD WEEK:
THE TIME OF THE FORERUNNER

The second period of Advent is marked by the figure of John the Baptist. He is featured or mentioned in all the Gospel passages. The first readings, however, do not always relate directly to the Gospels. This is sometimes the case, but long passages of Isaiah continue to be read during this period.

THE BRIDEGROOM'S FRIEND
When we speak of John the Baptist, we are at once reminded of eschatological expectation, which originated with the ideology of kingship in Israel and was rooted in the people's conviction that Yahweh was faithful. For the believing Israelite, God was a rock, a refuge offering hospitality and a shield. The fulfillment of this eschatological hope is also presented in the Old Testament as a replica of the act of creation: Yahweh will create "new heavens and a new earth" (Is 65:17; 66:22). Man will be restored to the first glory of Adam. Before this takes place, however, the people will experience a new exodus. Just as the conquest of the promised land had been preceded by a long journey through the desert, so too will the people withdraw into solitude before approaching the end time.

With this in mind, it is not difficult to understand why, during the period immediately preceding the Christian era, most religious communities insisted on their members being trained in the desert. This requirement is reported, for example, in Is 40, the fragment with which the work of Second Isaiah begins and which, together with its parallels, seems to have inspired later Judaism.

But who was to inaugurate the eschatological era—God or his Messiah? This question was discussed in all Jewish circles, and each group was convinced that, if it were a Messiah, he could only be born within that group. The Pharisees, John the Baptist and his followers and indeed every group had its own idea of the one who was to be sent by God.

John should be seen as part of the spectrum formed by these different groups. But, as Luke points out so clearly, he was above all a gift of God.

His mother had been barren for a long time, like Sarah, Hannah and Samson's mother before her. Those women had in their old age given birth to sons who were in a sense heroes and at the same time signs of God's unchanging presence with his people. John too was such a sign of God's presence, and in addition to being a forerunner he also had the task of reconciling (see Mal 3). He preached conversion and tried to form the people of the new exodus. He regarded the rite of water baptism that he adopted for entry into his community as the seal of a change in his new followers' way of life. The Messiah whose coming he proclaimed was to be a judge with the task of dividing the good from the bad.

Jesus was among those who received John's baptism and joined his movement. Like the other disciples, he also preached and baptized. Did he quickly prove himself to be in a certain sense superior to his Galilean companions? He certainly soon came to be regarded by some of them as a rival. There is a significant reference, for example, in the fourth Gospel to some of John's disciples warning their leader, when he was baptizing at Aenon, about what they interpreted as competition. The Baptist's reply was immediate: "The bride is only for the bridegroom; and yet the bridegroom's friend, who stands there and listens, is glad when he hears the bridegroom's voice. This same joy I feel and now it is complete. He must grow greater, I must grow smaller" (Jn 3:29–30). John knew that he had run his race and had only to bear supreme witness. At Macherontis, he could have told the executioner: "He is the Lamb of God."

THURSDAY OF THE SECOND WEEK

IN PRAISE OF VIOLENCE

Is 41:13–20: Stirrings in the Near East—the Persian tornado overturns empires and nations take fright and look to their gods for protection, but in vain. Israel has nothing to fear. Yahweh has raised up Cyrus the Great to deliver the people from captivity. Until now they have been buried among the Babylonians and like a corpse eaten away by worms. But soon they will rise up from their mortal remains and like a threshing-sled crush the mountains into powder. Rejoice, you chosen people of God! Your punishment is ended. The desert will put on its festive garments for you and the steppe will be covered with different oils. Rejoice and know that the hand of your Redeemer will do this!

Ps 116 is a hymn thanking God for his tenderness in taking the wretchedness of his people on himself.

Mt 11:11–15: Tradition has it that Elijah did not see death, but was taken up into heaven in a chariot of fire and will return at the end of time to inaugurate the kingdom. John the Baptist's preaching therefore makes the people hope that God is once again speaking to his people. They have the impression that time is approaching its fulfillment and that John is really the new Elijah.

It is not long, however, before a dispute begins between the disciples of John and those who follow Jesus. Is the Baptist the Messiah sent by God to prepare the event at the end of time or is he only the forerunner? The covenant concluded by Jesus is in fact superior. John the Baptist is greater than all the prophets, but he is less than any disciple in the kingdom.

"Since John the Baptist came, up to this present time, the kingdom of heaven has been subjected to violence and the violent are taking it by storm." This statement is enigmatic and recalls Mic 2:13: "He who walks at their head will lead the way in front of them: they will open the breach, they will pass through the gate and go out by it; their king will go on in front of them, the Lord at their head." The medieval commentary on this text was: "The one who leads the way is Elijah and the king is the descendant of David." Elijah, then, has come back in the person of the Baptist and Jesus is the Messiah-King. Those who follow him will take the kingdom by force.

■

"The kingdom of heaven is subjected to violence." Were these words in the Gospel interpreted in a purely moral sense during the centuries of insipid faith in an attempt to render them less harsh? You have to make a number of sacrifices if you are to enter the kingdom of God—inner, moral sacrifices—and you have to lead an ascetic life. But this interpretation does not do full justice to the statement.

In Isaiah we read: "The poor and needy ask for water and there is none; their tongue is parched with thirst." Is it not scandalous that

the violence of faith is so slow to help them? The kingdom of God is, after all, not a drawing room for pious souls. It is surely a desert in which God walks at the head of the exiles to lead them to freedom. There is a great violence in that God and he gives his people power. "Poor worm—puny mite," the prophet calls them, but God will turn them into a threshing-sled to "crush the mountains" and "turn the hills to chaff." He is called their "redeemer" and that title sounds like a challenge to fight.

God's struggle changes the desert into a rich, fertile garden. Man should in God's name struggle to transform the poverty of the poor into human dignity. That may be the violence of the kingdom. If it is true that "the least in the kingdom of heaven is greater" than the greatest of the prophets, then is it not also true that man's dignity in God's sight calls on us to fight in the struggle of love—a love that is far from being sickly sweet?

■

For men thirsting for life and dignity
  we pray, Lord:
make us eager for justice and love.

For people crushed by oppression
  we pray, Lord:
fill our hearts with the violence of truth.

For prophets committed to fighting for hope
  we pray, Lord:
increase their faith from day to day.

FRIDAY OF THE SECOND WEEK

JOIN IN THE GAME!
Is 48:17–19: Oracles of salvation and words of reproach alternate in Chapter 48. Israel has turned away too many times from Yahweh and has

been made unhappy because of this. The nation is, after all, saved by obedience to God's instructions. If it had been obedient, it would have enjoyed lasting peace and its descendants "would have been numbered like the sand"—"as many as its grains." That is what Yahweh promised Abraham.

Ps 1 is like a paraphrase of an ancient song of congratulations. The priest welcomes a man who has come to the temple to give thanks and congratulates him with the words: "Happy is the man who trusts in Yahweh." This poem was later rewritten by a scribe who turned it into a sapiential psalm by introducing the classical antithesis of the "two ways."

Mt 11:16–19: There is nothing new under the sun. Like all previous generations, Jesus' also does not know God's work. Speaking of eschatological salvation, the prophet Zechariah said that "the squares of the city will be full of boys and girls playing" (8:5). But Jesus' generation refuses to join in the game. It refuses to share in the joy of the Bridegroom, just as it had rejected the asceticism of the Baptist. There may be kids in the marketplace, but they are sulking like spoilsports. The boys refuse to dance when the pipes are played for the wedding and the girls are silent when the funeral rites are celebrated. But in the end, does it really matter? Divine wisdom is manifested in the works of Jesus.

■

Sufficient for the day is that day's trouble (see Mt 6:34). Today we mourn and tomorrow there is a wedding. You cannot dance from dawn to dusk. There is a time for playing the pipes and a time for beating one's breast, a time for the prophet in the desert and a time for drinking wine at the feast (see Eccl 3:1–8). Each day is an invitation on the part of God, and his word is rich enough to sustain hours of weeping and hours of dancing. But what is our response? We lose everything because of our spirit of contradiction.

What happens, then? We treat John the Baptist as one possessed because he leads an ascetic life, and we reject the Son of Man as a glutton because he eats with publicans and sinners. We describe one bishop as a communist because he is united with the poor in their misery, and another as a mystic and dreamer because he draws our attention to the primacy of prayer. What happens is that we are refusing to abandon our pre-conceived ideas. Surely we should rely on the "one who is coming," yet we make so many excuses for rejecting his appeal. We do not really want anyone to guide us.

A sulky child is a child who denies his very being as a child. Are we not, all of us, just naughty kids, victims of our adult sulking? Happy is the man who joins in the game. As soon as he does, full of eagerness to experience the adventure of living, he will feel, beyond all comfortable security, the wind of the God who is coming.

∎

Yes, Lord, you are the one who is to come.
We have looked for you in places where you were not
    and we wanted other signs.

But now we believe it is your word
    that draws us along, disturbs us
    and calls us to share in the adventure
    that will only cease at the end of time.

SATURDAY OF THE SECOND WEEK

A WHIRLWIND OF FIRE

Sir 48:1–4,9–11: Jesus ben Sirach was a distinguished citizen of Jerusalem writing at a time when the "ecumenical" attitude of Hellenism was a threat to the very existence of Judaism (c. 180 B.C.). His work is a hymn in praise of the revealed law. Why, he asks, should the Jews envy the achievements of Greek thought when they are in possession of authentic Wisdom?

Chapters 40–55 are a eulogy of the ancestors, but behind the persons of these men of Israel it is God himself who is being praised. The Jews continue to remember their ancestors because they let the Spirit of God be active in them. Elijah, for example, was a prophet of fire, condemning the irreligious attitude of the kings of Israel and defending Yahweh's honor against the priests of foreign cults. God therefore took him up "in a whirlwind of fire" and put him "on the reserve list" for messianism. He was to return at the end of time to prepare for Yahweh's visit.

"Rouse your strength, Lord; come to us and save us!" Israel's lament is heard clearly in Ps 80—the people are sorry for their wrong behavior. They ask God to come back and uphold them. This psalm is now the prayer of the Christian asking Christ to be present in his life.

Mt. 17:10–13: Elijah has come in the person of John the Baptist. John's words have disturbed a certain petty ruler and the prophet has therefore suffered the same fate as his predecessors. Jesus cannot expect to be treated differently, because martyrdom forms part of the prophetic ministry.

■

John the Baptist was beheaded to please a young dancer and because he had denounced a spineless petty king's adultery. What an apparently stupid way for prophets to die! An absurd and tragic fate, yes, but it may mysteriously reveal the irreconcilable conflict between the fire of jealousy and the passion of the word. What was there between Herodias and the Baptist? Was it not the struggle of truth? Yes, John was undoubtedly the prophet Elijah who had come back to earth—a glowing fire, an uncompromising word and a passion for God.

Elijah's life was a life of fire. His words burned like a torch and brought down fire from heaven. The prophet himself was taken up into heaven "in a chariot with fiery horses." Jesus once said: "I have come to bring fire to the earth and how I wish it were blazing already." It was to blaze, but it was to be the fire of love taken to the extreme limit. Passion for God was to be the passion of the crucified Son of man.

There is no other fire than that of love. But you must be on your guard against letting its glowing heat cool down and die and calling love what is no more than a comfortable warmth. A king told a young woman: "Ask for whatever you want and I will give it to you." A man said to God: "Let it be as you, not I, would have it" (Mt 26:39; Mk 14:36; Lk 22:43). The fire is very close to going out when love becomes weakness and cowardice. But love is reborn when a man hands himself over to God with a will that purifies all things in the

fire of passion. How happy those who are really passionate! Herod was not one of them.

■

Place on our lips, Lord,
 a word of truth that is faithful to the end.
Place in our hearts the fire of passion—
 the passion with which Jesus your Son
 handed over his life for us,
 to tell us the name and the cost of love.

MONDAY OF THE THIRD WEEK

THE AUTHORITY OF THE SPIRIT

Nm 24:2–7, 15–17a: Balak, a Jordanian king, sends for the soothsayer Balaam and asks him to curse the tribes of Israel who, under the leadership of Moses, want to cross his territory and enter the promised land. But Balaam feels a strange power enter him. He becomes ecstatic and pronounces two oracles of salvation over Israel. It is not difficult to imagine how the Israelites were comforted by this proclamation of a land covered with cedars and aloes.

But one question remains: What is the "star" that rises? Whose reign does it greet—Saul's or David's? Or does it welcome the coming of the Messiah-King whose star was one day to rise in the East? The oracle of Balaam was increasingly interpreted in a messianic perspective. Matthew used it in his story of the magi (2:1–12).

The structure of Ps 25 is alphabetic and it is related to the psalms of individual supplication. The ways of the Lord are love and truth, it tells us, as soon as man puts his trust in God.

Mt 21:23–27: "What authority have you for acting like this?" Does this take us back to the time of Balak and his unruly astrologer? Jesus' driving the dealers from the temple was an act of religious reform. The priests were angry because they believed that they alone were responsible for order in the sanctuary. So Jesus reminds them of John the Baptist, whom the people regarded as a prophet. If the priests recognized the authority of the forerunner, they would also have to recognize Jesus as the one who makes the kingdom of God a reality. But the Sadducees do not value John's baptism and cannot reply to Jesus' question. The debate ends on a note of refusal, and the unbelieving priests will not enter the promised land.

■

"Speak out, prophet! Prophesy, soothsayer! But do not dare to say anything other than what we are expecting to hear." How many prophets have ended by being imprisoned, tortured and put to death because they have let the Spirit speak in them—speak words that are unexpected, astonishing and not at all in accordance with the ideas of the established authorities. John the Baptist was put in prison and beheaded. Jesus was brought before Pilate in the praetorium and crucified. And it is still happening.

John's baptism was not a rite of purification like the others. It pointed to a change of heart, a radical commitment to God, an openness to the new era and a recognition of the Lamb of God, a baptism given in the Spirit and in fire. The people clung to it. The authorities protested against it.

But when God wanted to speak freely and when he wanted to express what was new in his coming, he filled an exceptional man with his Spirit and led him into the desert. He even let him become ecstatic when the need arose and filled him with words that were quite the opposite of what the scribes and Pharisees were expecting to hear. Those whose hearts were upright recognized a new authority in Jesus. But let us make no mistake about it—he was at first regarded as provocative and as a disturber of the peace.

It is, however, not enough simply to become ecstatic in order to say God's words. Mystification is dangerously close to prophecy. The priests' distrust of Jesus is understandable. How is the problem to be solved? The tree can only be judged by its fruit. Balaam's prediction would be valueless if the star that he proclaimed did not lead us to the birth of that poor man in whom God's word was made authentic.

Yes, we have to judge the tree by its fruit—and the tree laden with the fruits of the Spirit will always call the cross to mind.

∎

You cheer the hearts of your people, Lord.
Your star rises in heaven
  and your good news is heard on earth.
Continue the work of your hands today,
  so that your Church may be the prophet
  of a new future
  in which eternal brightness shines already.

TUESDAY OF THE THIRD WEEK

A LITTLE REMNANT

Zeph 3:1–2, 9–13: The period during which the prophet Zephaniah was living was especially dramatic. All the nations of the fertile crescent were dominated by a succession of conquerors—Assyrians, Scythians and Medes. Living in the narrow Palestinian corridor, Israel took part in political intrigues stirred up in an attempt to shake the hegemony of the dominant powers. A revolution against the Egyptophile party, for example, led to the enthronement of an eight year old boy, Josiah, and placed the country in the hands of Assyria.

Zephaniah reacted against the Assyrians' seizure of power and the religious syncretism that followed it. He spoke out against Jerusalem and its leaders, those "proud boasters" who were deaf to the word of God. The humble, on the other hand, he comforted. He is above all the prophet of messianic joy, and the poor could recognize themselves in his "humble and lowly people and those who are left in Israel seeking refuge in the name of Yahweh."

Ps 34 is addressed to God as a prayer of thanksgiving. Yahweh has heard the believer's appeal and has set him free from his anxiety. "Taste and see," all you who are listening, "how good Yahweh is!"

Mt 21:28–32: Jesus once again turns to the priests who, faithful to their own traditions, refuse to believe in him. They do not know the way to the kingdom. But the publicans and prostitutes, ignorant of the precepts of the law, were drawn to John the Baptist and believed in his words. Well, Jesus asks the priests and us as well, what do you think of it? Who will be the first to enter the kingdom of heaven? In any case, it will not be those who say "Lord, Lord" (see Mt 7:21).

∎

The publicans were certainly not respectable people. Officially they collected taxes, but it would not be far from the truth to call them public thieves. As for prostitutes, it is hardly necessary to describe them in detail. However much we meditate on these Gospel stories, we shall never cease to be surprised to find these men and women leading the procession into the kingdom of God. They would themselves also be surprised. I know, of course, that I ought to be more subtle and not simply apply one situation to another. Nonetheless, the Gospel does show us again and again that God's grace does not, in its boundlessness, recognize our human systems based on "good habits." God is really only interested in one thing: the faith that we place in his word of salvation. It is that which the Bible calls "poverty."

But how can we be poor if we know we are rich in virtues? How can we call on God if we place our faith in our own strength? The publican is not made righteous because he has stolen, but because he has believed in the one who invited him to follow him. In the same way, the saint is not canonized because he has acquired a large number of merits, but because he has believed in the grace given by the one who saves the poor. John the Baptist was feared and hated by the priests and elders because he welcomed everyone and required no more than heartfelt conversion. He did not trouble about the past life of those who were converted. But let us admit it: right-minded people are very rarely converted.

When Jesus came into the world he was recognized by shepherds. Make no mistake about it—those shepherds were in no way "respectable" people. The scenario is always the same in the Gospel. A little remnant welcomes the Messiah—a remnant composed of the poor, people whom we call nowadays the "less well off" or the "disadvantaged."

■

We bless you, Lord, at all times
   and ask that your praise may always be on our lips.
May the poor hear and rejoice.
One of the poor has cried to you
   and you hear him.
   You save him from all his troubles.
Whoever looks at you will shine—
   his face will be untroubled and clear.
You are close to the broken-hearted
   and you save those who are in distress.
Happy is the man who looks for you.
We bless you
   with all the humble and little ones,
   because you are good and you save us.

WEDNESDAY OF THE THIRD WEEK

THE SCANDAL OF THE GOSPEL

Is 45:6b–8, 18, 21b–25: Yahweh chose a non-Jew to set his people free—a choice that inevitably threw Israel into confusion. The prophet therefore had the task of providing an explanation. He does this by reminding his listeners of God's rights. God, the only Lord and Creator of the universe, has no accounts to render to anyone and he is also the God of the pagans as well as the God of the Jews.

He has also never hidden his intentions—he has always spoken through the prophets. "Send victory like a dew, you heavens, and let the clouds rain it down." Spoken by Isaiah, these words simply point to the end of Israel's exile, but for anyone with an understanding of the Scriptures, they are a marvelous promise of an era of justice and love.

Verses 10 to 13 of Ps 85 are an oracle pronounced by God at the conclusion of a prayer in which Israel asks him to give life and happiness back to the people.

Lk 7:18b–23: "Happy is the man who does not lose faith in me." The word used here is "scandal"—"who is not made to stumble and fall because of me." The choice of Cyrus was disconcerting and so is the way in which Jesus thinks of his mission. John the Baptist looked forward to a man who would restore justice and who would, as it were, clean out the stables. But Jesus speaks of mercy and in being merciful does what the prophet Isaiah said that the Messiah would do (Is 61). So Jesus' reply to John's question disconcerted the Baptist. What, then, did John decide? Did he cease to dream about a Messiah and put his faith in Jesus or did he continue to cling to his own ideas? "Happy is the man who does not lose faith in me."

■

Perhaps the greatest enigma that confronts us in the Gospel is this: How can we reconcile God's omnipotence as the Creator of all things with his infinite mercy and fatherly love of man? John the Baptist's doubt about Jesus is that of the believer who is on fire for God, but who has not yet heard the authentic message of the Gospel. The good news is, after all, not there for a hypothetical mankind. It is a proclamation of salvation, peace and happiness for all men, ordinary people, the blind, the deaf and the poor. What use is God's omnipotence if sinful and wretched men who are at the end of their tether are crushed by it? The scandal of Jesus is that he is both the one sent by God and the one who sat at table with sinners.

But it is so easy for us to misinterpret the Gospel. Jesus heals the sick in the New Testament stories and we at once put our trust in him. But what troubles us is that he heals so few people today. If we are to understand why the believer is blessed—"Happy is the man who does not lose faith in me"—we have to look at the problem from a different perspective and recognize that when Jesus was carrying out his mission, the sick were sinners—people with whom no one wanted to associate. In healing them, Jesus ran the risk of discrediting himself. At the same time, however, he also gave a new image to God's omnipotence.

That power was love. It was tenderness, pity, mercy and patience. God did not create the earth for it to be a desert. Anyone reading the account of creation with understanding will know that the rain is justice, the dew is hope and the rainbow is peace. Anyone who understands the word of God knows that Jesus is love of the poor. In him "love and loyalty meet, righteousness and peace embrace." In that encounter, he is the Son of God. The poor are at the heart of the Gospel, and Christ asks us: "Will you ever understand that my Father created heaven and earth for you to make them into a kingdom of peace for all men?" So: happy are the poor and "happy is the man who does not lose faith in me."

■

Heaven, send down your dew!
We pray for this, Lord,
  with those who are dying in our deserts.

Clouds, make justice rain down on us.
We pray for this too, Lord,
  with those who have been condemned
  without having been heard.

May our earth bear fruit.
We ask you, Lord, to open our hearts
  to those aspects of the world
  in which your face is seen
  in the suffering of the oppressed.

THURSDAY OF THE THIRD WEEK

PASSIONATE LOVE
Is 54:1–10: "Does a man cast off the wife of his youth?" Can that wave of love that filled the heart, those kisses exchanged and those intimate words

spoken be forgotten? Yet Jerusalem, the beloved bride, betrayed the trust her God put in her, preferring the illusion of easy idols to the firmness of a demanding love. So God left her for a while.

But now she can rejoice and increase the size of her tents to accommodate her children. She will no longer be called barren. She can forget the "shame of her youth"—the exile in Egypt—and the "curse of her widowhood"—the period spent on the banks of the Euphrates. God will call her as he did the first time, when she was no more than a child, and will overwhelm her with tenderness. The rainbow will replace the flood water, and the old covenant, which God has never broken, will be extended to include all the nations of the world.

Used at the feast of Hanukkah, on the anniversary of the dedication of the temple, Ps 30 expresses the thanksgiving of a sick man for his healing. He goes up to the sanctuary to thank God and invites his friends to share in his happiness.

Lk 7:24–30: Who was John the Baptist? What made the crowds come to hear him and respond to his appeal? The desert was not the court of Herod Antipas. There were no fastidiously dressed, daintily mannered courtiers there, bowing in front of the throne like "reeds swaying in the breeze."

John was a prophet and even more than a prophet. Through him, the kingdom of God entered the world. He was God's messenger, proclaiming the end of time. But those who listened to him were above all those whom Israel regarded as sinners.

■

If you are looking for lines to include in an anthology of passionate love, you need look no further than Is 54. We have no reason to doubt that these are words spoken by one who loves totally, simply because God is the lover and such passion is not worthy of a serious deity. Let us be honest—our knowlege both of God and of love is very incomplete. We call on a deity that is as dull as a day when the sun does not shine, and we live often without letting our hearts be filled with the passion of love. Sometimes we claim that we are loving, but we are really devoting ourselves to all kinds of substitutes, condemned by religious people in the name of Almighty God. We still have a great deal to learn.

But what is the point of departure for these questions about the Baptist? It is that "the least in the kingdom of God is greater than he is." This is not a devaluation of the prophet, but a true evaluation of the state of things as God wants them to be. For him, an unimportant little man is more valuable than a treasure and a poor woman is more precious than a queen. Splendid clothes are nothing, because God covers every one of his creatures with the cloak of his tenderness. What he values most of all is that men and women should be truly alive. He prefers the way of life of nomads wandering ceaselessly in the desert to that of Pharisees absurdly dressed in their dignity.

Reread the Book of Isaiah. Reflect about God's anger because his people had forsaken him. God is alive. In the depths of his heart, he knows what passionate love is. He swears an oath of eternal love and overwhelming passion. His love is more powerful than the mountains and more stable than the hills. God is a lover of a kind that has never been seen in the world—but how are we to know him if we hide away from the storms of that love?

■

God, you made life
  to break out in fruitful showers.
  Look at our barren, sad existence.
Open our hearts to your voice,
  speaking to us of love.
Teach us how to walk
  at the pace of your tenderness.
Then we shall know how to live
  and to give thanks without ceasing,
  praising the covenant
  of your love for us
  for ever and ever.

FRIDAY OF THE THIRD WEEK

INDIRECT LIGHTING
Is 56:1–3a, 6–8: The prophet is speaking here to fellow Israelites. They have returned from exile in Babylonia and are beginning to resettle in Jerusalem. The question of the admission of "foreigners" to their community has arisen and especially those who had not permanently settled in the country. Third Isaiah is faithful to the spirit of his predecessor and wants to welcome non-Jews. In his opinion, everyone who is faithful to the covenant deserves to belong to the chosen people. He has only to observe the law and the Jewish customs, especially the sabbath rest, to be invited into God's dwelling place on Mount Zion. The sabbath was particularly important—this law had been so well observed in Babylon that it had enabled the Jews to be distinguished clearly from the pagans in that land of exile. The God of Israel was not content, Third Isaiah teaches, simply, to bring the exiles home. He also wanted to restore the unity of mankind.

Ps 67 is a psalm of blessing. Using the language of a hymn, it expresses Israel's thanks to God.

Jn 5:33–36: John "came as a witness to speak for the light. . . . He was not the light, only a witness to speak for the light" (1:7–8). John recognized the Messiah and had even sent some of his disciples to him. But not everyone accepted his testimony. The Pharisees had been skeptical and had not accepted Jesus. Most of John's disciples had continued to follow their own master. Nonetheless, Jesus' testimony was superior to John's, consisting, as it did, of signs accomplished in the Father's name. Jesus' "works" were better than John's declarations. They showed clearly that the kingdom of God was present in him. Despite their clarity, however, men still had to be alert to what they revealed.

■

We have to be careful not to look directly at the sun. Light is not an end in itself, in any case. Its purpose is to illuminate what would not be seen without it. There are many examples of such indirect lighting in the Gospels. John is a "lamp alight and shining" illuminating Jesus. Jesus is the light, yes, but a light to reveal the Father, who is

invisible, a light beyond all light. And when Jesus calls on us to be the light of the world, he also stresses the work that has to be accomplished. "I am the light"—what a foolish thing to say! But Jesus only makes this claim in reference to the Father.

Faith too is a light, but everything depends on its orientation. Properly directed, it illuminates what is invisible and enables it to be interpreted. Wrongly orientated, it only reveals emptiness. But who will give our faith the direction and meaning that reveals God? A certain disposition, possibly, an openness of heart, making us trust in the one who bears witness and his works? The religion of the Pharisees is seen to be a source of lack of faith, because it keeps man firmly in a state of self-sufficiency. The good will of the little ones, on the other hand, is open to Jesus' signs, because it is based on a longing to live and to go further.

Think, for example, of the extreme case of the man who has ceased to know what night is. In the end, he sees nothing at all. He is quite different from the man who has fully explored the darkness. Every time day breaks, he is intensely aware at the first glimmer of dawn of still sleeping forms of life slowly awakening and approaching him.

Jesus did not do the works of God in the blinding light of illusory strength. He spoke of God in the gentle, humble light that revealed the Father's love without imposing it. That light was for faith and it was the light of faith.

∎

Continue the work that you began in the Church, Father,
  with the extraordinary man, John the Baptist,
  your Son's forerunner.
Let us follow him and, like him,
  be lamps alight and shining,
without imposing anything on our brothers
  but the humble light of your love
  revealed in Jesus Christ our Lord.

THE OCTAVE BEFORE CHRISTMAS:
THE TIME OF GIVING BIRTH

From December 17 onward, if the need arises, the series of days numbered according to the weeks of Advent is abandoned in the liturgy and an octave preparing directly for Christmas is celebrated instead. In the office of the hours, this octave is distinguished by the singing of the great "O" antiphons. These striking lyrical texts contain beautiful symbols of our messianic hope. To give but one example:

> O Rising Sun,
> you are the splendor of eternal light
> and the sun of justice.
> Come and enlighten those
> who sit in darkness
> and in the shadow of death.

These antiphons are now included in the lectionary of the Mass, where they are used as Gospel acclamations. The liturgy of the word is also based from December 17 onward on the Gospel accounts of Jesus' infancy. It is worth looking quite closely at these.

THE INFANCY GOSPELS;
SYMBOL OR REALITY?

The infancy Gospels are not factual historical reports, nor are they fairy stories. They reveal a very deep understanding of Christ. Neither Luke nor Matthew intended to write a biography of the child Jesus, but each of them wanted, in his own way, to say "yes" to that child, as the new Moses, the Son of David and the Son of God. Each wrote an account of what faith, inspired by the Spirit, had disclosed to the Church. After the Easter event, the disciples of Jesus did not look at him as they had done before. Each disciple had the task of contemplating the mystery of the risen Christ and understanding his mission. The infancy Gospels are therefore extremely Christological in content.

What the Spirit had disclosed to the Church had, however, not only to be understood—it also had to be handed on to others. But how could the inexpressible be expressed? How could that experience, rooted as it was in the resurrection of the Lord, be communicated to others? Like all the other biblical authors, the evangelists were confronted with the problem of language.

They solved this problem with consummate artistry. Both Luke and Matthew had a deep understanding and knowledge of Scripture and non-biblical writings, and both were able to employ symbols. So, when the star marks out the journey of the magi, it greets, as it does almost everywhere in the Ancient Near East, the coming of a king or a god, it fulfills the ancient oracle of Balaam, and it does something even more subtle—it pierces the darkness of the night and proclaims a great light shining on "the people that walked in darkness" (Is 9:1). When Mary goes to visit her cousin Elizabeth, King David and the whole of Jerusalem go with her and, with John the Baptist, express their great joy that the new ark of the covenant is approaching their walls. When Jesus replies with such astonishing understanding to the scribes, he is anticipating the later controversies that will take him to the cross.

Symbolic language is not the poor relative of literature. It replaces the language of reason when that is impotent or silent. Symbols conceal and reveal at the same time. Moses' hesitant approach to the burning bush is an example of man's endless search for the Absolute. The fire that does not consume the bush points to God's love, which respects the creature.

An excellent example of the symbolic use of language can be found in the world of the cinema. In a scene in the Italian film *La Strada,* Gelsomina is downhearted, and her companion, the clown Il Matto, tries to reason with her. But he appeals less to her mind than to her feelings. Taking a stone, he says to her: "Even a little pebble is useful!" Images and symbols are words that can be seen. They are a wonderful way of discovering the depths hidden behind the appearance of things and beings.

Scientific language can only reveal part of reality. The rest is suggested by symbolic language, because it speaks to man's imagination. That is undoubtedly why the infancy narratives so rapidly became part of the heritage of mankind and inspired the work of so many artists and writers throughout history.

DECEMBER 17

THE NEW MAN

Gn 49:2, 8–10: This passage contains a traditional biblical image. Conscious of approaching death, the patriarch Jacob gathers his sons around him and "reveals" the future to them. The text in fact originated at the time of Isaiah. It describes the situation of the tribes and particularly commends that of Judah, which will, according to the tradition of David's coronation at Hebron, provide the royal lineage.

It was not long before it acquired messianic overtones. The lion of Judah came to symbolize the royal Messiah, who would take his place in the midst of the assembly with the insignia of power "between his feet": "The scepter shall not pass from Judah, nor the mace from between his feet." The "prophecy" would be fulfilled in the Book of Revelation, with one of the elders acclaiming the Lamb sacrificed in the name of the "Lion of the tribe of Judah" (Rv 5:5).

Ps 72 is a royal psalm proclaiming the notion, common to most primitive people, that the king was responsible for the well-being of his subjects. He obtains salvation for his people and the prosperity of his country depends on him.

Mt 1:1–17: The original title of the Gospel according to St. Matthew is: "The book of the genesis of Jesus Christ." This title was, of course, taken from the beginning of the account of the descendants of Abraham (Gn 5:1). Matthew is saying here that Jesus is the new man, the key that opens the door to an understanding of the history of salvation. The division of the descendants of Abraham into fourteen generations is so regular that it would seem to indicate that history was governed by heavenly calculations. The attempt to achieve this regularity has, however, led to errors in the lists of names. It is clear, then, that it was not Matthew's intention to provide an exact genealogy. He wanted rather to include Jesus among the agents of the messianic promises and to link him especially to David. The number fourteen is important because it is the total formed by adding the numerical values of the consonants contained in the Hebrew name David.

But, unlike similar Jewish genealogies, this one includes the names of four women. Their presence can be explained by the need to emphasize Jewish traditions concerning their providential part in the development of messianic hope. Tamar, for example, is the woman who wanted at all costs to share in the blessing granted to her father-in-law Judah (Gn 38). Mary, whose name occurs at the end of Matthew's genealogy, is the woman through whom the promise was fulfilled. Because of his legal father, Joseph, Jesus is an authentic Son of David.

■

So-and-so was the father of so-and-so . . . Genealogies refer to the past and they give the impression that the only meaning of the births that they list is to overcome death, toward which each person is inescapably moving. Mary was the mother of Jesus. What does this mean? Surely that at a precise moment in our own times, a birth no longer pointed to the past, but took place as an eternal present in which the future of man was rooted. "To all who accepted him he gave power to become children of God, to all who believe in the name of him who was born . . . of God himself" (Jn 1:12–13). And man too is born of God in Jesus Christ, even though he is born from a man and a woman.

The new man, however, still belongs to the line of human beings, even though he is "born of God himself." God creates the new world on the history itself of the passing world. What, then, are we to say about these three sets of fourteen generations? What does the history of holiness tell us? Surely only stories of men and women who were not very holy. Tamar is often mentioned in this context. She was hardly the glory of the family of Judah. And David's relationship with Uriah's wife is not an example of moral behavior. Jesus Christ's ancestors do not give the impression that they have descended in a straight line from God.

Yet the list had to be drawn up. Christ did not simply come down from heaven. The Messiah was the fruit of hidden work in which God writes straight, but with curving lines. He carries out his plan of salvation using man as his partner in a work that goes far beyond him.

The genealogies could be extended beyond Christ, at every level—from his physical family with James of Jerusalem to his spiritual family with Peter of Rome. Would this provide us with a more flattering portrait? The history of the Church is the story of how a new world and a new man has been begotten throughout the ages. It is a history of man and a history of God. The Spirit is at work in it. He does not despise any earthly reality, even when he does something that transcends our earth completely.

What we have to do, then, is to compile our Christian genealogies with an eye to the future, in faith and hope and in the knowledge that, where there has been death, there will be even more life. We have to learn to see history not as an eternal recurrence of man's ancient fate, but as the mysterious progress of God's loving plan. Tamar and David, whom we condemn for their faults, may well have helped in secret to build a kingdom where God recreates man by forgiving him.

DECEMBER 18

EMMANUEL

Jer 23:5–8: The first of the oracles was pronounced when Nebuchadnezzar was interfering more and more in Judah's internal affairs by setting on the throne of David men who would serve him. The last of these rulers in order of date was the prince, Mattaniah, to whom Nebuchadnezzar gave the name of Zedekiah (meaning "Yahweh is our justice"). Was the reign of this puppet disputed? We do not know for certain, but Jeremiah undoubtedly stressed the legality of the monarch as a descendant of David. This is clear from the phrase "righteous branch" which means "legitimate." This text was originally not prophetic and simply formed part of the enthronement ritual.

The second of these two oracles looks forward to the end of Israel's exile. The return of the exiles is seen by the prophet as a new exodus. It is worth pointing out here that Babylonia was situated to the east of Palestine, but the path of the invasions of the country and therefore that of the new exodus ended, according to this text, in the north of Israel.

The name Zedekiah lends itself to a messianic interpretation. Was it not expected of the heir of the kings of Judah to gain the support of the people in his concern for justice and unity in the country? This is obviously the theme of Ps 72.

Mt 1:18–24: A righteous man, Joseph belonged to the race of Simeon and Abraham, to the lineage of all those anonymous men who were the bearers of Israel's hope of the coming kingdom. Matthew is quite delicate in the way in which he stresses Joseph's part in the mystery of salvation. Just as Jesus did not claim equality with God, Mary's husband did not claim the right to be called the child's "father." He welcomed Christ as what he really was: a gift from heaven. He also welcomed Jesus in his own lineage and, in obedience to the angel, gave him a name. The prophecy was therefore fulfilled and a legitimate "branch" took possession of the throne of David.

■

"Joseph, son of David, do not be afraid!" But what would he fear? We should not for a moment think that he might have been mistrustful of his wife, suspecting her of infidelity. He was a righteous man—in other words, a man who had God's faithfulness in him. No, what he feared was that he might take up a place alongside Mary and Jesus that did not go back to God alone. The child came from the Holy Spirit, but God, in his faithfulness, also required that he should be the "Son of David" as well. So: "Do not be afraid, Joseph! Take your place alongside Mary. Give the child a name and be a father to him."

What is being a father to a child? It is having a relationship with him from day to day, adopting him and being adopted by him in a relationship that will never end, loving him and being loved by him in growing freedom that looks forward to the child's future adult life.

Jesus experienced that relationship. Even his name indicates that— Jesus meaning "God saves" and Emmanuel meaning "God with us." God cannot, after all, save us or be with us without having experienced our history and our everyday life. Jesus does not save us by a miracle. He is our Savior because he was truly human. At that level, Joseph has an indispensable place in the history of man's salvation.

Joseph is the man who adopted the Son of God. He is righteous because of that. We shall also be made righteous in the same way when we learn how to live, at the heart of our hesitant love, the history of Emmanuel, God with us.

■

We pray for parents here on earth:
  may they welcome their children
  as a gift of your grace.

We also pray for those whom you call
  to serve you:
  may they be committed in faith and simplicity.

When we are astonished by your presence
  and invited by your word
  to go forward, we also pray:

Be with us, Lord, Emmanuel!

DECEMBER 19

BARREN WOMEN
Jgs 13:2–7, 24–25a: This pericope can be regarded as one of the models that inspired Luke when he wrote his account of the annunciation. Barren women paradoxically play quite an important part in the history of salvation. On the one hand, they draw attention to God's extraordinary power and, on the other, they point to the fact that their children are a gift of God to mankind. Mary's story appears at the peak of biblical history

and transcends all other parallel stories, since she became fertile in her virginity.

Ps 71 is a psalm of supplication, emphasizing God's support of the man who prays to him from birth onward.

Lk 1:5–25: The source of Luke's account of the birth of John the Baptist was probably priestly traditions. These authors were no doubt very proud of the part played by Zechariah's son. A powerful argument in favor of this source is the precision with which the evening sacrifice is described by Luke.

The scene takes place within the impressive framework of the sanctuary. But the literary framework provided by Luke is no less important. With John the Baptist, God renewed his relationship with his people and broke a silence of several centuries. The vision of the seventy weeks, which comes from Dn 9, is present everywhere in Luke's infancy Gospel. The angel Gabriel consoles the visionary during the evening sacrifice by announcing a messianic era to him. Then, when Jesus' parents bring him to the temple (Lk 2:22–28), they do so seventy weeks after Zechariah's vision had taken place.

The mission of the Baptist is described in the prophecy made to Zechariah in language borrowed from the prophet Malachi. "With the spirit and power of Elijah, he will go before him (the Lord) . . . preparing for the Lord a people fit for him" (cf. Mal 3:24). When Zechariah leaves the temple, he is not able to bless the people outside, because he is dumb. He is, however, like his barren wife Elizabeth, righteous. Both of them are images of Israel, the recipient of the blessing given to Abraham who was not able to hand on that blessing because of his sins. The people have therefore to wait for the coming of Jesus, the child of the promise, for the heavens to open again. Risen again, he will bless the new Israel in his disciples.

∎

While the people were praying in front of the temple, the priest entered the sanctuary to offer incense to the Lord. Would God speak that evening? If only he would tear open the heavens! But he had been silent for too long and, although men continued to pray, he seemed to be elusive. The people were barren. When would the earth once again yield fruit? The priest himself was very old and childless. He would soon die. He remained silent in front of the altar.

"Zechariah, your wife Elizabeth is to bear you a son." The old man is so astonished that the angel goes on to praise the child who is to be born. At last Zechariah is able to speak again, but his first words are an objection to what he has heard: "How can I be sure of this?" In other words, "How can that be? I am an old man and my wife is old." The angel's reply might have been: "God will bring it about in his usual way, Zechariah. He makes the desert fertile and renews men's hearts. He has heard his people's prayer and he will answer it in his own way, according to the fullness of his grace. The child will be called John, that is, 'God is gracious.' And you, skeptical priest, will remain dumb until everything has taken place in accordance with God's word."

God has broken his silence. Darkness has been replaced by light. Soon a voice will be heard in the desert preparing the way for the Word made flesh. And God, who is "enthroned on high," has leaned down over the poor and "enthrones the barren woman in her house by making her the happy mother of sons" (Ps 113:5, 9). The unbelieving man is reduced to silence because, when God is gracious, only faith can sing the evening canticle, the song of the rising sun, proclaiming life beyond the darkness of night.

■

May our prayer rise up to you, Lord,
  like incense,
and may our hands be raised to you
  like the evening sacrifice.
Speak to our barren hearts
  and let what you say be done to us
  according to your grace,
  on the morning that you give us
  as a new day born in our faith.

DECEMBER 20

THE HOUSE OF SILENCE

Is 7:10–16: Ahaz, the king of Judah, is experiencing one of the most difficult periods of his reign. His neighbors, threatened by invasion by the Assyrians, are urging him to join them in a defensive alliance. Ahaz, however, is more inclined to seek protection from the invader. Isaiah has always rejected any suggestion of an alliance with a foreign power and tells the king to rely on Yahweh and to ask God for a sign. Claiming that God should not be put to the test as his excuse, the king, who is really afraid to put his trust in the Lord, refuses to do this. Isaiah rebukes Ahaz, then proclaims the sign himself: "The maiden is with child and will soon give birth to a son whom she will call Emmanuel."

What exactly does this oracle mean? Is the child Prince Hezekiah and is the young woman the royal bride, as many have believed? Is Isaiah simply saying that the dynasty will, despite all the dangers that threaten it, survive? If this is what it means, the prophet is merely repeating the ideology in favor in Jerusalem: that Yahweh is faithful to the promises he made to Nathan. This may be so, but it is impossible to overlook the mythical overtones of Isaiah's language. The Immanuel who is to be born is that marvelous king to whom each of the countries of the Ancient Near East looked forward and who was expected by Israel more than by any other because of the promise made by God. The sign can be found above all in the name of the child: "God with us." God is always with his people in every crisis.

Ps 24 is related to the canticles of Zion and outlines the conditions required for admission into the Lord's house.

Lk 1:26–38: "Rejoice, so highly favored! The Lord is with you." The angel speaks to the young woman of Nazareth using the words of the prophet Zephaniah, who had called on Jerusalem to rejoice because God had repealed its punishment and was ready to live within its walls. That was, however, something that the holy city would experience in the distant future, whereas Mary is to become the mother of the Messiah, who is to sit on the throne of David, in the immediate present. She is, in other words, to receive in her own person the eschatological visit proclaimed by the prophets.

"The Holy Spirit will come upon you . . . and the power of the Most High will cover you with its shadow." On the one hand, there is the Spirit and, on the other, the cloud: the Spirit of the world's first morning, when life, rising up out of the original chaos, left to conquer the universe; the cloud in the desert—the sign of God's presence for his people. Mary is the new ark of the covenant, the one who is especially favored by God. She is greater than Sarah and Elizabeth, because the child she is bearing is the Son of God.

▪

Everything has taken place in silence, in recollectedness and in reflection about the mystery. God has come among men in a peaceful house unknown to tourists. Gabriel has left the temple built by men to announce the birth of God in the authentic house of David, known only to God. Since that time, God has made a habit of this. His infinite mystery can only be expressed in the house of silence. The good news that those whom he has sent have brought to us and the fruits that his Spirit causes to grow in us can only be understood if we are recollected.

Mary is quite disconcerted. How can the silence of her virginity give birth to the Word of God? How can a humble servant—a "handmaid"—be the mother of the eternal King? The words of God are disconcerting and we can only bear them within us, without dying of fear, if we are silent. They are words of truth and they are about to become a reality—in the inner recollectedness of a young woman who suddenly finds herself fruitful. The Holy Spirit seizes hold of her like a morning breeze, in a mystery that cannot be known. The power of God covers her with its shadow—very discreetly, so that the body of the Son of God can develop within the fragility of that human being.

From that time onward, Mary's silence was to become acceptance, obedience and faith. She was to let the fruit of God grow within her and bring to it the only form of sharing that God can really bless— total faith, humble and full of joy. David, the ancestor, had dreamed of a magnificent and enormous dwelling place for God, a home worthy of the Infinite One. But God "pulls down princes from their thrones" and "sends the rich empty away" (Lk 1:52–53). He wants to

dwell with the poor and the lowly. He entrusted his Word to the one who liked silence enough to avoid identifying it with talk. God needs our silence because he wants to make what is impossible a reality for us. Shall we, then, be able to welcome his Spirit with as deep an inner recollectedness as Mary, the faithful virgin, when she said: "Let what you have said be done to me"?

■

Blessed are you, Lord, in the honor of the Virgin Mary,
   for her silence welcomed the immensity of your Word.
Your Spirit made a covenant with her
   and in her heart she conceived the one who contained the universe.
Available to the mystery that you had prepared for centuries,
   she handed over her life to serve your Word.
This is why our hearts are full of joy and cheerfulness
in your presence, God—you who exalt the lowly—
and why we bless you for ever.

Emmanuel, God with us, Jesus our Savior,
   be with us, Lord!

Son of David and Son of Mary,
   be with us, Lord!

Rising sun, dawn of peace, seed of justice,
   be with us, Lord!

God our Savior, we bless you!
Your love begets the unexpected one
   and our earth bears its fruit
   in Jesus, your child.
Let us preserve these things in our hearts
   until we can give you endless thanks
   for ever and ever.

God, holy one,
   we praise you.

Our lives were like a desert,
  but you remembered us.
A woman welcomed hope
  and her flesh trembled with joy
  at the breath of your Spirit,
  so that the child should be born.
God, you do marvels.
  We praise you for your grace.

DECEMBER 21

SPRINGTIME DANCE

Sg 2:8–14: A rabbi has stated: "What a wonderful day when the Song of Songs was given to Israel! All inspired Scriptures are holy, but the Song of Songs is the holy of holies." It is really a collection of songs for a wedding and throughout it praises human love. It is full of a sense of wonder at the constant newness of that love. The young man asks the girl to join him, and his longing for her is like the springtime in Palestine, both fiery and fresh. The whole of nature is involved in it—it is the season of love. The turtledove is cooing in the field and the sun is ripening the fruit on the trees.

These words too were written by someone who understood human love: "Of all the sacred texts, the Song of Songs is the one that has convinced me most of all that the constancy of lovers helps God." The young man's impatience expresses God's zeal for mankind. Very soon the Song of Songs was interpreted allegorically as praising the mystical wedding between Yahweh and Israel.

But the God of tenderness is also the God of the dance. He "shouts for joy" (Zeph 3:14–18a) because the exiles are coming home. And in Ps 33 we read: "Happy is the nation whose God is Yahweh."

Lk 1:39–45: Let Jerusalem rejoice as when David danced in front of the ark and all the people were happy (see 2 Sam 6). You too should dance,

Elizabeth, since your house is not a tomb. Soon it will echo with the cries of the child who is now leaping with joy in your womb. Dance too, Mary, for you have found favor with God. Run to your cousin and bring peace to her. Go into her house. It is close to Jerusalem, the city that killed the prophets. Sing, Mary, since the tomb will not be able to hold the Prince of life.

■

"Winter is past, the rains are over and gone. . . . The season of glad songs has come. . . . Come, then, my love!" She comes at once and Elizabeth's house is full of joy. The barren woman has stripped off her garment of mourning. She is dancing with joy, spurred on by the child dwelling within her and the Spirit inebriating her. The Day has come.

Mary greets her cousin and Elizabeth becomes ecstatic. Joy is everywhere in the house because it comes from the one who is coming into the world to give birth to joy. Mary sings, inspired by the Spirit animating her child. Elizabeth exults with the joy of the forerunner who has not yet been born. John the Baptist expresses his joy already—even before he has been born. Joy is born of the promise. It is given to us when we come to life like the child born of hope.

Yes, joy is born of the promise. It makes us look ahead of us. Because of it, we look further ahead in faith. The barren woman is in her sixth month of pregnancy and there is no need now, with spring ahead, to think about the winter. Mary is in our midst like an icon of faith, both hands wide open to receive each day as it comes. The one who will live in the grace of faith will dance every evening. He will feel the Spirit and life itself trembling within him, even when everything seems barren.

Each believer bears Christ within himself. Faith has meaning only when it gives birth to life. Mary's virginity is fruitful, but our fruitfulness is not so much a physical one—it is rather a gift of life that rises up in us when our lives are handed over unreservedly to the Spirit of God. Happy is the man who has the Spirit dwelling within him and who can sing in faith: "My lovely one, come! Show me your face . . . for your face is beautiful!" Happy is the man who can dance to the sound of a beauty that can only be revealed by faith.

∎

When you are with us, Lord,
  your Spirit trembles in our hearts
  and we praise you, exulting with joy.
Visit us, Lord; come to us
  and set us free from our barren lives,
  so that we may go forward on our way
  and invite others to join in the dance
  that will last for ever and ever.

DECEMBER 22

A CANTICLE FOR A REVOLUTION
1 Sam 1:24–2:1a and the canticle of Hannah (1 Sam 2:1, 4–8 passim): Hannah had been in despair because she was barren. She had therefore promised the Lord to consecrate to him the son that he was to give her. When Samuel was born, his mother went up with him to the temple and showed him to the old priest Eli. Then she thanked the God of life in a canticle celebrating the change in her situation that had brought her, as a previously barren woman, such blessing. "It was to shame what is strong that God chose what is weak by human reckoning" (1 Cor 1:27).

Lk 1:46–56: The Magnificat, the Benedictus and the Nunc dimittis—the Gospel of Luke contains these canticles. They have an aesthetic function, but that is secondary. Their primary purpose is to throw light on the events on the occasion of which they were sung. Jesus' birth has a very important meaning for mankind, but how often do we fail to look for that meaning or listen carefully to what the event is saying to us? Almost everyone perhaps so fails, apart from a few who are in the habit of listening to God's Word or have been visited by the Spirit.

When she went to Elizabeth's house, Mary was congratulated by her cousin. She understood very well the deep meaning of Elizabeth's words and she at once began to "magnify"—in other words, to "proclaim the greatness" of God and his work. She knew that the promise made to Abraham had been fulfilled in her, and her song was concerned with what she had discovered in the history of her people—that "God is with us" and that he was present in the lives of men and their struggles. "He has pulled down princes from their thrones and exalted the lowly." Setting Israel free from slavery in Egypt or sending prophets to destroy idols—it was the same God who did this and who refused to accept man's alienation. There is little doubt that the Magnificat originated among the "poor" of Israel and that it proclaims their ultimate exaltation. Behind Mary's faith and the humility of the Savior of Bethlehem are the poor and the hungry of the whole world. What the Magnificat is saying to them is that God is on their side.

■

A young woman sings a canticle for a revolution. The child she is carrying is to be the prophet of that fundamental change. The song of the world's poor is embodied in Mary, and the Spirit expresses in her the revolutionary faithfulness of the God who will raise up those whom the world despises. How often the Virgin has had to suffer because of our sweet and sickly presentation of her!

God "looked down on his lowly handmaid," and she did not, in a spirit of false modesty, apologize profusely. From that day onward, all generations have called her blessed. It is true that she was very young and that she did not know very much when she sang those words. But young people are very venturesome—and that is all the better for God, since it is God whom Mary is celebrating.

Let us listen to what she says: "He has shown the power of his arm, he has routed the proud of heart." The battle is on, and when Jesus comes to grips with the Pharisees, he will have difficult men to deal with. "He has pulled down princes from their thrones and exalted the lowly." Mary knew the psalms. They formed the substance of her prayer. That is very good, because she can in that way teach us how to pray. If we do not pray as she did, we are in danger of complaining like sinners without conviction, when we ought to be truly humble. Let us accept, then, that God can and wants to teach us.

"The hungry he has filled with good things." Mary experienced that hunger, that longing, that passion for life. But she did not say "yes" to God just for the sake of peace and quietness. Not at all. God knew that he would find that hunger and thirst in her and that was why he asked her to carry his Son.

That, then, is God's revolution. How wonderful that it began in a young woman. God's revolutions take us much further than our own breathless little struggles.

■

Blessed is she who believed in your word.
  Blessed are those who believe without having seen.
Your Spirit, Lord, always goes ahead of our expectations
  and your power is always stronger than our fears.
Let your Church welcome you, then,
  and may everything happen in our lives
  as only you can make it happen.

DECEMBER 23

GOD IS GRACIOUS

Mal 3:1–4, 23–24: History seems sometimes to be a perpetual process of beginning again. Malachi carried out his ministry about 450 B.C., a period when Israel had returned from exile and the temple had been rebuilt. The people, however, had soon returned to their old ways, and worship in Jerusalem had fallen to a very low level. The prophet Malachi reminds everyone of his responsibilities. He proclaims the coming of Yahweh and says that his judgment will be "great and terrible." The Lord himself will "enter his temple" and purify his priests, the "sons of Levi." His coming will be preceded by that of Elijah, who will have the task of preparing men's hearts for the kingdom. Jesus will testify to his disciples that this function was effectively fulfilled by John the Baptist.

Ps 25 is usually included among those psalms that express an individual complaint. It is written in alphabetical form, and the antagonism separating the righteous man from the sinner emerges clearly from it. It implores the Lord to teach the man whom he has loved from his youth onward the right way.

Lk 1:57–66: John means "God is gracious," and that is the name that Zechariah and Elizabeth gave their child, despite a certain disagreement. What a wonderful career lay ahead of the one who was later to find the Messiah among his disciples! A new world was born with John; something quite new appeared. Did the people of the hill country of Judah suspect that when the whole neighborhood echoed with the sound of rejoicing because Elizabeth had been blessed by God?

■

His old mother carried him in her womb for nine months, and for three she asked herself again and again: "How has this happiness happened to me?" The child she was carrying had leaped for joy, and his presence, becoming more and more overpowering within her, was the sign of the presence of the God who does wonders. Zechariah's dumbness continued, but gradually it changed into astonishment. Every day he meditated on the words that came to him when he was in the sanctuary: "His name will be John . . . God is gracious."

"When the time came for Elizabeth to have her child, she gave birth to a son." Eight days later, the child was circumcised in the presence of a great number of people and had to be given a name. That was the father's privilege and everyone expected the baby to be called Zechariah, so that the name of the father, who was now very old, would be perpetuated. With that name the child would take his place within the line and later become a priest like his father. His future would be assured by his name. So, like his father, he was to be Zechariah.

But no—he was to be called John. Called by grace, he was to have the name of grace "to give his people knowledge of salvation" (Lk 1:77). His name was to point not to a family line, but to an unexpected future—God is coming! God is gracious—"the rising Sun that is to visit us" (1:78). God is not in the past. He opens the way to the future. Birth is not a perpetuation of what was in the past, but a risk of faith in the future. God's grace is renewed again and again. John was to be the forerunner of God's grace, calling on men to go beyond themselves and forward to meet the future with its risks. Our God is coming. We must go on, even further, and encounter him.

■

You are gracious, God,
   and we bless you, because you renew all things.
Let us enter into the spirit of the coming feast
   as people welcoming a birth
   that bears within it the dawn of a new future.

You never reject your covenant, Lord.
We thank you for this
   with all the prophets
   who looked forward to the day of your coming,
and especially with John the Baptist
   who, for us, pointed to the Lamb of God
   and prepared in the desert
   the way along which we can meet you.
In the communion of the Church throughout its history,
   we acclaim your love.

DECEMBER 24

GIVE VOICE TO PRAISE
2 Sam 7:1–5, 8b–12, 14, 16: David has conquered the holy city and has had a palace built for himself—a "house of cedar" for the king of Israel and Judah. A grandiose plan begins to form in his mind—he will build a temple worthy of the God who has supported him in all that he has undertaken and centralize worship in Jerusalem. It was a great ambition for a great king, but he was not to have time to achieve it and the temple was finally built by his son Solomon.

He was more fortunate, however, in the dynasty that he founded. And Nathan, the official court prophet, was responsible for the rise of Solomon and became the one who interpreted God's favor for the king. David, who owed everything to God, was not able to build the temple, but Yahweh still strengthened the rule of those who succeeded him.

Ps 89 is a royal psalm celebrating the promise made to David that his line would continue. Its purpose may have been to lend support to the dynastic idea at a time of crisis, possibly when the kingdom was divided.

Lk 1:67–79: After nine months of silence, it was time for the word of God to mature in Zechariah's heart and for the old priest to become open to God's grace.

There is little doubt that it was originally the Messiah who was celebrated in the Benedictus, and Luke is really quite crafty in applying it to John the Baptist. In a sense, however, this is relatively unimportant, because the canticle is fundamentally a celebration of salvation in progress. The child who has just been born is, as it were, a foretaste of the other child to whom Mary gave birth and in whom the ancient promise made to Abraham was to be fulfilled. All nations were to be blessed in him, the "rising Sun from on high." In the words of the prophet: "The people that walked in darkness has seen a great light; on those who live in a land of deep shadow a light has shone" (Is 9:1). All the nations are included in this: the provinces separated from Jerusalem and for the time being under the yoke of Assyria and the pagan people whom Luke had the joy of seeing as member Churches.

■

"Zechariah's power of speech returned and he spoke and praised God." Doubt and fear had paralyzed him and he had become dumb. His dumbness had not been a meditative and recollected silence, but a mute impotence through which the Spirit was unable to break. He wanted a sign. He was an old man and he had forgotten Abraham and his barren wife. He did not want to venture on the way without an assurance that it was the right way. Then he was given the sign—nine months of withdrawal into silence, long enough for God to do his work and to make a man who would be the sign of his grace.

But God only condemns us in order to set us free. He worked patiently on the old priest and transformed his dumb silence into an inner recollectedness in which the word was born and grew. For nine months Zechariah ruminated on the word. Now we would say perhaps that he interpreted the event in the light of Scripture. So, when the child was born, he had no need to look further, and he knew that he was to become a priest of the new covenant. He no longer had to offer endless sacrifices. From that time onward, his task was to give voice to his people's praise.

We should listen carefully to him giving thanks to God: "Blessed be the Lord our God, for he has visited his people." Today salvation has come down into this house. He has set my words free. He has set his grace free. The time has been fulfilled and God has raised up his power in the house of David, remembering his promises and his faithfulness. "He has remembered his holy covenant, the oath he swore to our father Abraham," for those who put their faith in him.

"And you, little child . . . " You will be a prophet. You will prepare the way for the Lord. You will lead his people in the light from on high. You were conceived by the goodness of our God. You will bring peace to "those who live in darkness and the shadow of death."

Yes, the light has risen. The morning Sun has come to visit us. Our desert has been illuminated by a new day. Soon John will go out into the desert and will stay there until the day dawns when the one who is the true light for men, their life and hope, appears.

■

Such is the tenderness of the heart of our God
   that a morning Sun has visited us from on high.
Guide our steps, Lord, to the light of your grace,
   Jesus Christ, your child, your face.

THE SEASON OF CHRISTMAS

"Something that we have touched with our hands: the Word of life" (1 Jn 1:1).

"The Word was made flesh . . ." (Jn 1:14). Words fill our lives, jostling and pushing each other, trying to push one another out. But they also come together intimately and express the deepest mystery of our faith. God is love and tenderness, not severity or solitude—that is wonderful, surely, but is it not just a "way of speaking"? Then we say again and again: it is not just a word or words about God, but the Word who is in God that was made flesh—made flesh, face and history. No religion has ever jostled and pushed so insistently as Christianity in the endless search for God made by men since they were first created and first surprised by what went beyond their immediate understanding of their lives on earth. The Word was made flesh.

The Word—the Logos! What can we say about it? We have dissociated thought from speech and verbal expression, with the result that the inner word of human communication is often no more than an external sign, an effort with little or no reward or even a lie to which everyone more or less consents. How often do we say, for example, without even reflecting, as an excuse for our lack of precision: "What I really mean is . . ." and even then do not succeed in saying what we mean!

The Bible was fashioned within a people of flesh and blood, and in it the word is a source of life and strength. It is always unexpectedly new. It is powerful and has the fascination of magic. Centuries before the development of linguistics, the biblical authors had discovered what we now call the "performative word." That word goes beyond the expression of an objective content and is action, appeal, fascination or obstacle. Everyone knows that a word or phrase such as "I love you" is quite different from the everyday statement: "It is raining." When the Bible says of God: "He said . . . And so it was" (Gn 1 *passim*), it is expressing and raising to a very high level a human experience that every man can have so long as he does not speak in order to say nothing.

God speaks. God expresses himself, even though he is inexpressible. In God, the Word is the expression of being. In the beginning was the Word and that beginning was the absolute origin, because it is God himself. God exists in speaking. He is dialogue—*dia-logos*, the word exchanged, absolute communication and perfect communion. We have unfortunately isolated being in a solitude that cannot be reached, and that is why it is so difficult for us to understand the Trinity. The Trinity may be a mystery, but it is not a "problem," at least for the man who lives in the interpersonal face to face encounter that enables him to become what he should be. God is the dynamic Word. He exists by acting, so much so that his Word is consubstantial with him. It is another "he." "God said . . . And so it was." This has to be affirmed of God himself and not just of his actions in the world. God is because he expresses himself in his eternal Word.

We could stop here and contemplate this revelation, basing our faith on knowledge. That was the temptation to which the gnostics of the early Church succumbed, and those of us who refuse now to be really flesh and blood are tempted in the same way. But the Word was made flesh: not by a sort of condescendence, but by an inner thrust, an overwhelming love, a deep longing—and man was created in the image of God. What is the value of knowing God if that revelation teaches us nothing about man and if we remain shackled in our own unhappy history?

What God said was man, a history, a passion. A very small history, of course, of an Aramaean from an obscure part of the world, and a passion that was almost ridiculous and in the hands of very unimportant politicians. But "the Word was made flesh . . . and we saw his glory" through a Gospel consisting of stories, encounters, signs and parables. It was a day to day history, like our own.

The Word was made flesh. It was made flesh and became friendship and love of the brothers, the power of forgiveness and the tenderness of a look. The blood of a man flowed in his veins and living water from his heart. He visited Cana and he went to the cross. He encountered Peter and Mary Magdalene and he encounters you and me. God began to speak, after so many prophets, through the mouth of his eternal Son, who is the face of his glory. His word entered a man, but with the humbleness of an open face, through the lament expressed by a dying voice and in the passion of a man who risked everything at the risk of losing himself.

"Everyone who loves . . . knows God"—that is the song of the Apostle John (1 Jn 4:7). That knowledge is made of flesh and blood. The way of the knowledge of God will always be the roundabout one of human history and that of the histories of individual people. Since Christ's coming, there are no longer two sides: one of the eternal Word and the other of our stammerings. At the heart of the new covenant there is Jesus Christ, the Word of God and our flesh. The words that are on our lips are God's words. They are appeal and communion, cry and song. That is because the Word perpetuates in each individual person the history of Emmanuel, God-with-us.

The liturgy of the season of Christmas does not spend much time at the crib. It is a celebration of the incarnation and confronts us at once with the men and women who put their faith in Jesus: John and Mary at the tomb, Simeon in the temple and Stephen faced with death, Andrew, Nathanael, a fig tree, a dwelling, a crowd of hungry people in the desert, a leper on the road and Capernaum. Everything is flesh and blood.

Underlying all this are the many different emphases in the single message of the elder, John, in his struggle against gnosticism: "Something that we have touched with our hands: the Word of life"; "Anyone who lives in love lives in God" (1 Jn 4:16); "Children, be on your guard against false gods" (5:21).

May the celebration of the word and the bread strengthen in us each day not only our faith in God made man, but also our faith in man who is called to become a child of God—a man of flesh and blood. You are that man.

■

We thank you, Father of men.
   God, you loved the world so much
   that you gave your Son to it.
He is your face, shining with tenderness,
   and he shared our humanity.

*He was poor even at birth
  and he handed himself over,
  going to the very end.
In him, you tell us your word of peace
  and we know what you are for us.
With all those who have recognized
  your mercy and your glory in him,
  we praise and bless you.*

*Whoever walks in the light
  is in communion with God.*

*If we walk in darkness,
  we are not living the truth.*

*If we confess our sin,
  God will purify us and make us holy.*

Lord, enlighten our ways!

THE FIRST EPISTLE OF JOHN

Is there a thread that will lead us through the rich complexity of this letter and enable us to follow the continuous reading of it suggested by the lectionary? We can find that thread so long as we place the letter back in its original context and understand the author's way of writing and thinking.

Let us consider the context first. The letter was written in response to a concrete situation. John's community was divided because many believers were being led astray by false teachers: "Several antichrists have already appeared.... They came out of our own number" (2:18–19). These men were skilled in the doctrine of gnosticism, which they believed was superior, because it made it possible for God to be known directly, without the mediation of the incarnation.

John calls them "liars": "The man who denies that Jesus is the Christ—he is the liar" (2:22). These gnostics believed that Jesus could not be the "heavenly Christ." At the very most, the "heavenly Christ" could only have dwelt in him from the time of his baptism until his suffering and death. Knowledge of God or gnosis was the consequence of a direct vision of God, which had nothing to do with earthly or carnal realities. Gnosticism was therefore a superior form of truth and as such was opposed to the faith of the community of the Church that was based on a recognition that Jesus was the son of God. Gnosticism was in fact the first attack against the Christological teaching that was beginning to develop in the Church. At the same time, however, it also posed an absolutely radical question of faith: How are we to know God? How does God reveal himself?

What is the Apostle's response to this? His epistle, which was probably addressed to all the churches in Asia Minor, is not a doctrinal refutation of the gnostic heresy. It aims rather to strengthen the faith of Christians and to affirm the authentic truth. It certainly contains many such affirmations of faith, but although they are repeated again and again, they are hardly ever supported by arguments. The author's concern to put the Church on its guard against gnosticism led him to emphasize a number of truths. These are stressed more clearly and forcibly here than anywhere else in the New Testament. The epistle takes us up to a peak in the Christian revelation and can be seen as the result of deep reflection on the part of the early Christian community about the realism of the incarnation and the theological question of man's knowledge of God.

"Everyone who loves . . . knows God" (4:7). The letter stresses the extraordinary relationship between love and knowledge, "because God is love" (4:8). "If anyone acknowledges that Jesus is the Son of God, God lives in him and he in God" (4:15). This last statement points to the astonishing relationship between faith in Christ and living in God that is emphasized in the letter. This twofold conviction is, moreover, a single conviction because "God's love for us was revealed when God sent into the world his only Son, so that we could have life through him" (4:9) and "We have known and put our faith in God's love toward ourselves" (4:16). Faith and love, then, are the only way along which we can know God. The gnostics denied Christ

Jesus and caused a division within the Christian community. In so doing, they showed that they did not have a valid claim to a knowledge of God.

We must now turn to the author's way of proceeding, in other words, his style. One way of attempting to understand biblical texts is to distinguish different levels, often quite clumsily combined, but this method is not necessary here as the epistle has a very real literary unity. It is better in this case to observe how the author moves forward in spirals, dealing again and again with the same questions, each time throwing a new light on them.

One key phrase in the epistle is rendered in the older translations as "by this you know" or "from this we know." The author's aim is to provide believers with criteria of "truth" in order to arm them against the claims of the gnostics. For example: "You can tell the spirits that come from God by this: every spirit which acknowleges that Jesus Christ has come in the flesh is from God, but any spirit which will not say this of Jesus is not from God" (4:2–3) and "We have passed out of death and into life and of this we can be sure because we love our brothers" (3:14).

The author of the first epistle returns three times to this question of criteria. How do we know that we are "in communion with God"? The first exposition (1:5–2:28) is concerned with the theme of light: "God is light. . . . If we say that we are in communion with God while we are living in darkness, we are lying, because we are not living the truth" (1:5–6). The second of the author's expositions (2:29–4:6) describes communion with God in terms of sonship: "In this way (= by this) we distinguish the children of God. . . . Anybody not loving his brother is no child of God" (3:10). The third exposition (4:7–5:12) is that communion with God is sharing in the life of God. It may be, of course, that the author of the first epistle is not so much providing criteria as pointing to the foundation of Christian life: "Anyone who lives in love lives in God and God lives in him" (4:16), "because God is love" (4:8).

BETWEEN CHRISTMAS AND THE NEW YEAR:
WITNESSES TO THE LIGHT

There is strictly speaking no octave of Christmas because the feast itself lasts for a whole week. Only the celebration of Easter lasts in this sense for an octave. Immediately after Christmas are feasts that have always been associated with the incarnation because they celebrate the saints of the New Testament. These are followed by days of which Simeon and Anna bear witness to the Word made flesh.

Witnesses! The Gospel has already told us that the Baptist came to bear witness to the Light, but the same can be said of all those who were called to point to the Lamb of God. Stephen died as a perfect image of the Lord on the cross and so bore witness to the Son of Man, raised up in the glory of the Father. John, the beloved disciple, went to the tomb. He saw and believed, seeing in faith what the eye cannot understand. Even before they were able to speak, the children of Bethlehem were called to join Christ in the mystery of love that is mocked but still victorious. Simeon recognized the Messiah and sang in praise of the Light that his eyes had seen, even though they were already half-closed, and Anna rejoiced because her hope had been fulfilled. "The light has come into the world" (Jn 3:19; cf. 1:9ff) and it is life for those who welcome it.

During this season of Christmas, the Church continues to proclaim its faith in the Word made flesh. The Church's liturgy can help us, then, to be witnesses to that "light that darkness cannot overpower" (Jn 1:5). It is the light of faith: "If we live our lives in the light, we are in communion with God" (1 Jn 1:6–7).

∎

Whoever is born of God
  can no longer sin . . .

Whoever puts his hope in Jesus
  remains as pure as he is pure . . .

See what love the Father has for us—
  we are children of God . . .

God of tenderness,
  let us dwell in you!

DECEMBER 26
THE FEAST OF SAINT STEPHEN, THE FIRST MARTYR

A CHILD CHALLENGING DEATH
Why is the feast of the first Christian martyr celebrated immediately after Christmas? The reason can be found at the very origins of the Christmas cycle. The feasts of Christmas and the Epiphany were the result of theological reflection about the truth of the incarnation. The same theological consideration led both the Western and the Eastern Churches to associate the saints of the New Testament with Christmas and Epiphany because they were men who had in one way or another served the Word made flesh most closely. So we find the feast of John the Baptist celebrated before Christmas and, after Christmas, those of Stephen, James and John, the Holy Innocents, and even Peter and Paul.

Acts 6:8–10; 7:54–60: "The disciple is not superior to his teacher" (Mt 10:24; Lk 6:40). Stephen, we are told in Acts, worked "miracles and great signs among the people," just as Jesus had done. His words infuriated the members of the synagogue, who debated with him just as they had debated with Jesus, even when he was a child. Stephen was fervent and enthusiastic, and he was certainly one of the first to break with the Jewish past. He was a Hellenist and preferred to preach in synagogues reserved for Jews of Greek origin. He spoke as openly as Christ had done, denouncing the Jews' superstitious attachment to the temple and proclaiming that man was more important than the law.

It was not long before he was arrested. Jesus' trial was repeated. The same men accused him and there were the same witnesses. Even the accused man's defense was the same. The same words of trust and forgiveness were heard again at Stephen's trial, and his supreme testimony recalled that of Jesus: "I can see heaven thrown open and the Son of Man standing at the right hand of God." The disciple's death reproduced that of the Master.

Ps 31 reads like a cry for help. From the beginning to the end of this psalm we are aware of the trust of the persecuted man whose only refuge is the faithfulness of his God. There is, however, a glimpse of a happy ending: "I will exult and rejoice in your love."

Mt 10:17–22: There is darkness ahead. "Beware of men!" Do not trust even your brothers and the members of your family. The word of God is like a sharp sword (see Heb 4:12), cutting into man's heart and revealing his most intimate thoughts. No man can be indifferent to it. He may rebel against it or submit to it. He may retreat into his own pride or self-sufficiency, or he may look with sorrow at his own sinfulness.

At every period of history men have borne witness to the truth and right. Have they always known that the Spirit of God was speaking through them? Most of them have suffered the same fate. They have been put on trial and handed over to the executioner. They have endured so much suffering. But the supreme values of mankind, bearing witness to man's ultimate destiny, have been built on it. It is the solid, fertile ground in which the Church has taken root. Stephen died and Paul came to life.

■

How strange Stephen's fate was! If we are to believe Luke—and he is a reliable author with the greatest respect for his sources—Stephen was a Hellenist who was chosen to serve at table, in an attempt to settle an institutional difference that threatened to reduce the Church in Jerusalem to impotence (see Acts 6). But the word dwelt in him. It was more powerfully present in him than in anyone else. Was he the man of the New Testament in whom the word became most fully flesh and blood? There was, of course, Paul, but he was at that time still deaf and blind. Luke, the theologian of the Christian mission, was really very glad to present Stephen as the first missionary, the man who witnessed to the Word made flesh. The widows in the early Church had to be neglected. The word of God had priority.

Stephen spoke with the openness of a child. He disregarded all the precautions of oratory and the subtleties of diplomacy. In the presence of the high priest, his interpretation of the history of the people of God was a model of plain speaking, in which his intention was abundantly clear: to expose the vanity of the temple and therefore of the religion of the Jews, which had become institutionalized, identified with cultic practice and fossilized. The only form of worship that Stephen wanted was adoration of God the Creator and the "Son of Man standing at the right hand of God"—a religion in which God and man were face to face and in which there was no vain, useless mediation. Face to face with death himself, he was transfigured with glory. Another protomartyr, Irenaeus, said that "the glory of God is man alive."

This was a religion of the incarnation, a religion of man. And yet: "Beware of men!" The wars of religion have been the most cruel and the most inhuman. Jesus died at the heart of a religious conflict. He was born as a protest on the part of God, confronted with religions that connected his future to their own past. Men have denounced their fellow men and handed them over to the secular arm because of Jesus. The incarnation has always contained within itself man's recognition or his betrayal of his fellow men. But "when they hand you over, do not worry about how to speak or what to say. . . . The Spirit of your Father will be speaking in you."

What words does the Spirit speak? They are not words of defense or argument, but words that set the truth free: "Lord Jesus, receive my spirit. . . . Do not hold this sin against them." They are words that tell the truth about man when God dwells in him to such a degree that he has become one flesh and one spirit with him; they are words of a child, that is, of a man who is fully open to the future and free to forgive and to know God beyond the barriers of religion.

Throughout the whole of his life, Jesus lived as a child. He was constantly astonished and fascinated, free and entirely handed over to the Father and to men. He died as a child, in the vulnerable nakedness of a birth. Today men and women are handed over to death because they are brave enough to criticize the structures of this world with the clear eyes of children, and the high priests of our failed religions try to reduce them to silence by stoning them to death. Ought we not to pray without ceasing so that, when they are confronted by death, they will express, perhaps with their last breath, the testimony of the Spirit: "Father, forgive them; they do not know what they are doing" (Lk 23:34)? That is, after all, the only Word that God has chosen to save the world—a Word made flesh to the last drop of blood.

■

Jesus Christ,
 you came in the truth of our flesh—
 we adore you and bless you,
 because you are the Son of Man,
 standing in the glory of God the Father.
Word begotten before the ages
 in whom all things subsist,
 we give you our faith and our hope,
 because you are the truth
 in whom man discovers his future and his freedom.
Confonted with death,
 you forgave those who struck you
 and let the Spirit express through you
 words of reconciliation.
We pray to you today
 for those men and women
 who are martyred in the name of faith.
May they be one flesh with you,
 so that the testimony of their blood
 may tell the world the word of eternity
 that can only be expressed by silence
 in that vision of the life beyond
 in which you stretch out your arms to every love
 that is given to the very end,
 so that your eternity will at last appear.

DECEMBER 27
THE FEAST OF SAINT JOHN THE EVANGELIST

A GLANCE—A WORD

1 Jn 1:1–4: The unity of the Church! How impressive and resolute these words are: "What we have seen and heard we are telling you, so that you too may be in union with us, as we are in union with the Father and with his Son Jesus Christ." The unity of the Church—that was what the evangelist had in mind at a time when it was threatened by a dispute as old as mankind: Surely it is unthinkable that God should be able to suffer and die like an ordinary man. Even in the earliest days of Christianity, some people could not accept this, and this, of course, placed the reality of the incarnation in dispute. This question is still with us, since history repeats itself in insidious ways for every generation.

Everything is made explicit in the prologue to the letter: The Word of life—the Logos that the gnostics claimed to be able to know directly—was manifested in Jesus: "We have heard (it) and we have seen with our eyes; we have watched (it) and touched with our hands." This takes us back to the evangelical tradition, which is not a learned theory, but a history attested by witnesses. Jesus is the Son of God and in him we contemplate life "with the Father."

Ps 97 is one of a group of psalms praising Yahweh enthroned in honor. Originally it served to acclaim the glorious return of the ark of the covenant after a military campaign. It speaks of the enemy's terror in the presence of God's omnipotence and of the earthquake caused by his coming. But now we have no need to be afraid. God may still reveal himself on a mountain, but he has a human face—the face of a man transfigured.

Jn 20:2–8: Mary sees that the tomb is empty. She runs to the disciples, but has only something very commonplace to tell them: "They have taken the Lord out of the tomb." She is thinking of body-snatchers. She is not yet fully alert. She does not really believe. Yet she has sensed the secret promises contained in the lifeless body of the one she loved so much and very soon she will initiate a great deal.

Now, however, she still has a long way to go. She has first of all to hear the official testimony of the Church. Peter will be responsible for that as the first of the apostles, and he therefore assembles the evidence—the linen strips placed on one side and the "cloth that had been over his head rolled up in a place by itself." This is silent evidence, but is this not a time of recollection, when every object has the value of a sign pointing to what is invisible? The absence of the body is not a proof of the resurrection, but it does indicate that the body has not been forgotten by the glorifying power of the Spirit.

John is the last to arrive. He has, in a sense, reached the end of the road. He looks at the linen strips, but that is all. His glance is really turned inward. He is searching, yes, but in his memories and his own heart. The wine at the wedding feast, the temple cleansed, Lazarus—he senses what is possible in so many ways and yet unsuspected. An open tomb and strips of cloth, a woman and two men, the need to interpret—everything is very ordinary, but it has the value of a sign. "He saw and he believed."

■

A newly born child that his mother wraps in linen strips. An open tomb and the strips of cloth, the winding-sheets, carefully rolled up. Between these two events, a man like all other men. In the beginning, a handful of shepherds—poor men glorifying God for what they had seen. At the end of that man's history, the disciple whom Jesus loved—"he saw and he believed." So very little is needed for faith to be born. Very few things, but things that are as infinite as the heart and love itself and as deep as a woman's warmth and the silence of a mystery. The disciple went in and saw—"he saw and he believed." A moment later, Mary cried out with all her heart and the impulsiveness of her flesh: "Rabbuni!" And we too "give testimony" to what "we have touched with our hands." "We are announcing that message to you" (1 Jn 1:5).

"So that you too may be in union with us": that union is a communion of faith sealed by a little bread on our table and the hope expressed by our hands joined together in the language of peace. It is a very fragile communion, as easily damaged as a baby that has just emerged from his mother's womb and more mysterious than a tomb open to the silence of the absent one. It is a communion of love and praise that can be shattered very easily if it refuses to be simply a communion based on a contemplative glance. "What we have seen with our own eyes . . . and touched with our hands." The Word of life! The Word heard by the disciple when he let his head rest on the Master's heart during that farewell meal when love handed itself over and went to the very end. The Word that Mary felt entering so deeply into her being when, with her perfume, she proclaimed the hour of burial. The Word of life! "We are announcing that message to you."

"To make our own joy complete." How bold! But so few things are needed to make joy leap up, just as life made the stone closing the tomb move. So few things: the tenderness of a glance, the fascination of music, the peace of a friendly handclasp and, at the heart of all this, a source of life that transfigures our flesh, a word spoken by the Word of life, a word spoken by the Son of Man, a word of Love made flesh. The word spoken by Jesus to Mary: "Mary!" and to Peter: "Peter, do you love me?"

■

Jesus Christ,
  little Child who learned words very slowly,
  in the beginning you were
  the Word that gave birth to the world.
You were the most beautiful of the children of men
  and your face charmed the eyes of our hearts,
  but at the end of the day you entered the tomb
  and we have touched with our hands
  the coldness of your body.
Now we know you
  in the fascination of beauty,
  the tearful silence of our suffering
  and the stammering of our searching faith.
Jesus Christ,
  our Lord and our God,
  open our eyes and guide our hands,
  so that, in the communion of our hopes,
  we may find joy and peace
  beyond death
  in that daily giving birth
  that is the beginning of eternity.

God, whom no eye has ever seen,
  we bless you for the reflection of your glory
  made manifest in Jesus, your beloved Son.
Word begotten before all ages,
  he came to express your love for us
  and he lived among us.
Full of grace and truth,
  he gave us your forgiveness
  and he saves us from death.

DECEMBER 28
THE FEAST OF THE HOLY INNOCENTS, MARTYRS

SOLIDARITY WITH EXILES

1 Jn 1:5–2:2: The author's aim in writing this letter was to restore full unity in the Church—that communion that had been threatened by the gnostic heresy. He therefore sought to unveil the message of Christ, not because it was not known to those to whom he was writing, but because what it demanded of believers had to be known at a deeper level. What had to be done in order to be in communion with God? It was necessary to live one's life in the light (1:5–2:2) and to observe the commandment of love (2:3–11).

After the introductory words, then, the author states a fundamental demand of truth that always has to be observed by the believer. He denounces the gnostics' illusion that they are without sin and living in communion with God. What he probably had in mind was their claim to be morally superior, when in fact their morality was no more than a kind of sinless amoralism. They closed their eyes to sexual license, but at the same time despised the "flesh," by which they meant day-to-day living and brotherly love.

This attitude was quite wrong, because it was a denial of the truth. An authentically Christian attitude, John insists, was one of constant conversion and the confession of sins. If we live in this way, the truth will be in us and we shall "live our lives in the light" and be in communion with God. We shall also be without sin, because we shall be saved by Christ.

Ps 124 is one of the so-called "songs of ascents." It is basically a thanksgiving, but uses very realistic imagery to point to the dangers from which the believing people have escaped.

Mt 2:13–18: Are they symbolic, those children who were massacred in Bethlehem? Of course they are, but we should not forget that symbols are always rooted in human realities, and the reality here is that of human suffering—people dying of hunger, the bitter complaints of exiles and the silence of frightened prisoners. It is the suffering of Rachel weeping because the Assyrians had taken her best sons into a foreign country, and of Jacob-Israel driving his flock, so reduced by famine, to Egypt.

What is Yahweh's response to these lamentations? It is: "Stop your weeping, Rachel, dry your eyes. . . . There is hope for your descendants" (Jer 31:16). A child is coming from Egypt. Is it perhaps Israel escaping from Pharaoh's anger and preparing to cross the Sea of Reeds? Or is it the young Church, purified in the waters of baptism and the bath of persecutions? "Stop your weeping, Rachel"—God has preserved a remnant of the people. "I called my son out of Egypt." God's response to man's cries is to send his Son. He is called Jesus, "God saves."

■

Almost as soon as he had been born he was exiled. Nowadays children grow up in refugee camps and do not even know the meaning of the word "home." Sometimes children have to be adopted so that they are able to call someone "father" or "mother." There is a very long list of little exiles. Jesus was one of them.

We should not forget that the history of the people of God began in a concentration camp—in Egypt, which is seen in the Bible as the symbol of all slavery. The history of that people took real form when a liberator became conscious of the misery of his fellow countrymen and led them through the desert in a long exodus. The history of God is written with immense patience and care. We are right to denounce the Herods of history and to reject violence and terrorism, but are we sufficiently acquainted with the inner violence that is the pre-

condition for peace and that we should feel when we hear the cry of the oppressed and see the misery of those in exile?

Faith is a life of wandering and not a settled existence. How did the angel deal with Joseph? He did not reveal the future to him. He simply gave him an order of the day: "Go!" "Come back!" "Go to Nazareth!" Each day a new order—"each day has enough trouble of its own" (Mt 6:34)—a kind of exile without any certainty for the future and no reassuring plans. Faith is a constant state of exile—placing oneself in God's hands as though one were in the desert, learning how to live in communion with Jesus Christ, in solidarity with strangers and exiles. There is no abiding city for the Church on pilgrimage, but just getting up in the middle of the night because a cry is heard—the cry of the innocents and the cry of the innocent one who took on himself the sin of the world on his long way of the cross.

∎

Nothing is more painful than a maltreated child.
Do not let us remain indifferent, Lord.
Open our hearts to what we have so far ignored,
   since your Son assumed
   the face of a rejected child.
Shake us out of our torpor—
   we have no abiding city
   apart from your kingdom
   for ever and ever.

For parents preparing for the arrival of a child
   and for those who are tested by loneliness—
   we pray to you Emmanuel, God with us.

For those exiled in a distant country
   and for those who have the peace of a home—
   we pray to you, God, who call us to unity.
For those who have been awakened to the adventure of each new day
   and for those who are closed in their nostalgia for the past
   we pray to you, God, rising Sun.

DECEMBER 29

THE ENCOUNTER

1 Jn 2:3–11: The second step in John's letter shows us how opposed he is to the attitude of the gnostics, who are so sure of their "superior knowledge" that they are able to reject the yoke of God's commandments. They pride themselves on knowing God better than those believers who keep faithfully to his word. John, however, is convinced that they are "liars" and that, in the way that they behave, they have separated faith from everyday living.

The true believer observes the law of God, which can be summed up in the one commandment of love. In this, John's letter echoes the fourth Gospel. This commandment of love is both old and new. It is old because it is rooted in the living tradition of the Church and it is new because Jesus showed in his own death on the cross the depths at which man must live when he is called by God.

Ps 96 is an invitation to praise God. When he "comes to judge the earth," the whole of creation will "tremble before him."

Lk 2:22–35: "Seventy weeks are decreed for your people and your holy city, for putting an end to transgression, for placing the seals on sin, for expiating crime, for introducing everlasting integrity, for setting the seal on vision and prophecy and for anointing the holy of holies" (Dn 9:24). Today the time for the encounter has come. God has entered his temple and has come to live among men. His coming is, however, not proclaimed on the drum and the trumpet. He comes as a child carried in his mother's arms, as a first-born consecrated to the service of God, which is also the service of men. Driven by the Spirit, Simeon goes forward to meet him and blesses God. The old man contemplates God's glory and is now able to die in peace. The old Israel is going to make way for the new covenant. But Simeon also sees God's glory on the way to Jerusalem, where death is already visible. God is visiting his people and the judgment has already begun. The child is there "for the fall and for the rising of many in Israel." God comes as a sign and Mary, the daughter of Zion, will be torn by the drama of her people.

■

Jesus moves unnoticed among the immense crowd in the temple. The priests are too busy with the religious rites to be aware of anything. Mary and Joseph form such an integral part of the crowd that God is able to come to this encounter incognito. But, among the people, an old man and an old woman are praying quietly. They are also waiting—for the Messiah. They are waiting and hoping, with the infinite patience of old people, and cannot be discouraged. Their eyes are already half-closed with old age, but they recognize the Lord and go to meet him.

Christ always comes to us quietly for an encounter with us. Today he comes as a little newly born child. Tomorrow he will come as quietly as a friend knocking at the door. In the evening he will beg us to look at him exposed naked on a cross. He will come again later risen from the dead. He will appear, but we shall not be able to hold him and he will disappear again just as we recognize him.

Simeon goes forward to encounter him. Driven by the Spirit, he takes him in his arms. This is not done according to the rules, because Simeon is not a temple priest. But true faith goes further than such rules. The old man is giving us an example, because the son of God always comes to meet us so that we may take him in our arms and become one with him. He comes so that we shall encounter God, and to do this properly we have to put the whole of our heart into the meeting. It is very likely that the angry crowd demanded his death because he again and again invited us to live our faith with our hearts and not simply rely on others for it. There are only two attitudes that I can have when I encounter Christ. I can either love to the point of death—that is the "new commandment"—or I can refuse to love. And that means I shall call for Christ's death. An encounter with Christ always strips the coverings away from our hearts and exposes them, naked, to the full light.

Our faith is like a sharp sword piercing us to the heart. There is the faith of Jesus himself, coming to do his Father's will. There is Mary's faith—she "pondered in her heart" (Lk 2:20) and also followed the way to Calvary. Finally, there is the faith of Simeon, the believer singing his Nunc dimittis. The old man carried the child, but the child guided his steps. "If anyone wants to be a follower of mine, let him renounce himself" (Mt 16:24).

In isolation we seek in darkness,
   and the night has closed our hearts to love.
But you, Lord, are light—
   a new light to guide all people.
So guide us! Open our eyes
   so that all your children
   may walk in the light of your Son,
   Jesus Christ, our Lord.

DECEMBER 30

THE OLD WORLD HAS PASSED AWAY
1 Jn 2:12–17: We have seen how the gnostics liked to think of themselves as being "without sin" because their morality was superior. And we have also seen how John condemned them: "To say that we have never sinned is to call God a liar" (1:10). Now he turns to true believers and tells them: "You have already overcome the evil one."

His aim here is to strengthen the faith of these believers. They are living in the truth. It is the others, the gnostics, who are in error. In preserving the Church's faith they are welcoming God's work in themselves, and in putting their trust in Christ they have an "advocate" with the Father. They, then, and not the heretics, have life. They should persevere in spite of the diabolic forces that threaten the community.

Ps 96: see December 29.

Lk 2:36–40: "Anna, the daughter of Phanuel, of the tribe of Asher": names were important in Israel. They expressed the destiny of the people and disclosed the history of the world.

Anna is "God is gracious." God has set his tent in the midst of the people. He has held Israel in his lap and coaxed him. He is full of grace for man and for the Son of Man who has come today into his temple. He has let his favor rest on him (see Mt 3:17; Mk 1:11; Lk 3:22).

Phanuel is "God is light." Rejoice, people of God! Today a light has shone on you. A star has arisen in a new heaven and the angels have sung: "Peace to men who enjoy God's favor" (Lk 2:14). So rejoice, people of God! An old woman has spoken about the child to "all who looked forward to the deliverance of Jerusalem." And they all heard her—she was, after all, a daughter of the tribe of "happiness."

∎

The old world has passed away. The old world, with all its longings, is disappearing. The old prophetess is aware of that—she has lived in it for eighty-four years. The time of longing is ended. And yet it is not quite over, because she has been living with one great longing. Throughout her years of serving God, she has been longing for the day of the Lord. She, as the daughter of the God of light, has never been able to let the light of her heart go out until she had seen with her own eyes the light from on high.

She has spoken about the child to everyone she has met. She seems to have begun a completely new life. If it is true that the old world has passed away, then a new world must have been born. It has indeed been born here on earth, yet surrounded by a halo of light from on high because it is the world of Jesus Christ who has come in our flesh. Our flesh and all that we have longed for have been given meaning and a new life in him, but the world—the old world—does not understand.

"Nothing the world has to offer . . . could ever come from the Father," the apostle tells us. Then he outlines what the world offers: "the lustful eye, pride in possessions" and selfish longings. But he is not condemning life—he is giving a new orientation to creation that has been disorientated by sin. "My own children," he says, "you have already overcome the evil one." May your selfish desires be transformed into a burning desire to share and a longing for peace. May your "lustful eye" be changed so that you see God's face in everyone's face. May your possessions be a source of unexpected happiness for those who have nothing. God's word in our heart is a call to live a new life and to be young again so that the world may be reborn. Would anyone not want to spend his life with this longing in him?

*There is no darkness in you, Lord,
  and anyone who looks at you
  is surrounded by your light.
You are life,
  the source of translucent light.
Teach us how to see you as you are.
Bathe us in the clarity of your grace.
Then we shall live in communion with you
  and long to love one another
  in the new world that you have created
  so that it will last for ever and ever.*

DECEMBER 31

ALPHA AND OMEGA
1 Jn 2:18–21: "They will all know me, the least no less than the greatest" (Jer 31:34). The author continues to appeal for serenity. He did not know, any more than anyone else, when the last hour of history would come, but, like all the members of the early Church, he was certain that the hour would be preceded by the arrival of antichrists, who would try to draw believers away from the truth.

And those antichrists are already present. They were originally part of the Church community before beginning to preach doctrines that are contrary to faith. There is good reason for those who are still faithful to be disturbed, but they may rest assured. They have, after all, received the good news and they have been anointed. May they persevere in faith, then.

Ps 96: see December 29.

Jn 1:1–18: Although it has a strict theological unity, the prologue to the fourth Gospel consists of several different elements, corresponding to the various aspects of the Johannine traditon.

The first section (verses 1–5) is a fragment of a hymn reinterpreting in a very original way the first chapters of Genesis. The Word is seen as subsisting eternally with God and as occupying a place of great importance in the work of creation. But sin entered the world when the first man fell and, separated from the Word, creation once again became the nothingness of Genesis (1:3). Everything was through him, but, separated from him, creation again became nothingness. The darkness could not, however, prevent the entry of light, because the light was superior to the darkness. There is a certain dualism in these first verses of the Gospel, and they probably reflect the thought of the Baptist's followers and form a pre-Christian hymn.

Verses 6–13 are directed against John the Baptist. After Jesus' death, the early Christian missionaries encountered many of John's followers, who continued to regard him as "the light." So the evangelist's text stresses that the prophet was only a man who had been commissioned by God and that, while he was bearing witness to the light, that light came into the world. But the true light was received neither by the world nor by the Jews. The triumph of the light was therefore limited by man's free choice and his refusal to be open to God's grace. But Christ gave to all those who recognized his light the power to cross from the camp of darkness into that of light.

Every trace of dualism is absent from the concluding verses (14–18). The light is not opposed to the flesh. On the contrary, he became flesh. That incarnation is the decisive moment in the history of salvation. In Jesus, men can contemplate God's glory, and Easter morning has revealed the mercy of the Father and his faithfulness to his promises. In this third section of the prologue, the theme of the word is reinterpreted in a clearly Christological sense.

The word that has come from the mouth of God will not return to him, the prophet Isaiah declared (45:23), without having had its effect on men. As in the beginning, then, it took flesh and did creative work. It made it possible for a handful of believers to become children of God. The manna in the desert was not the real bread of life, nor could the Mosaic law give men "grace and truth." It was no more than a shadow of the Word made flesh in Jesus Christ.

■

"His own people did not accept him" (Jn 1:11). God's poverty became his drama. He came to his own people and, like anyone else, looked for a welcome and accommodation and expected to be understood and encouraged. God comes every day to his own people, but we close the door to a God who does not live according to the rules and will not admit a Word that throws our thoughts into confusion. Christmas is also a feast of conversion. The Word became flesh, and only God knows how much that cost him. The way from the manger leads to the cross.

And yet "he gave power to become children of God to all who believe in his name" (Jn 1:12). To all who believe in Jesus the Savior, the God of sinners, the lost, the humble, the God of tenderness. To all who believe in his name, who are aware of the light in the darkness of the night, who hear the word in the silence of a faith that is always threatened. And to whom did he give that power? To the Samaritan woman, the man born blind, a group of sinners in Galilee and those who were at the foot of the cross. To those people he gave power to become children of God.

They were born of God. They came into the world just as Jesus had come and they are still being born, those sons and daughters of poverty and insecurity with no other support in this world than God, his love and his Spirit. They come into this world, and their life is a journey. They are pressed by time to continue along the way. They are very fragile and are reborn again and again, called to be children of a God whom no one has ever seen. They are nameless, stateless orphans and exiles—at least according to the world.

According to the world too, a year has passed. Tonight people will wish each other a "happy new year" without knowing whether it will be or not. Shall we, children of God, be able to face the future with no other luggage than our faith? It is, after all, our faith in Christ that distinguishes us from all the antichrists who want to lead us astray on ways that are not those of the Word that is new every day. Only Christ is the Alpha and the Omega, the beginning and the end. It is not because antichrists are called "children of God" that we follow them on a way that is different from that of God-with-us, the Word made flesh in the humility of our flesh.

■

You are always greater than our plans
   and your purpose goes beyond our expectations.
Your Son was begotten by your Spirit
   and by the same Spirit you renew our lives.
Come to us, Lord;
   let us be reborn in your Word.
   Open our hearts
   and respond to our hopes
   today and every day for ever.

Today we wish each other happiness in the new year.
   Let us entrust those wishes to the one who will hear them
   and take them further than we dare to hope.

We entrust to you those with responsibilities—
   may they bear witness to that which they are the first to experience.

We entrust to you those who are able to promote peace—
   may they commit themselves firmly to the service of others.

We entrust to you the happiness of our partners in marriage,
   the future of our children, the health of our sick
   and the fulfillment of all our plans—
   may we seek what is best in all things.

Increase our faith and strengthen our hope,
   that we may be men and women
   according to your Word.

BETWEEN THE NEW YEAR AND THE EPIPHANY:
THE BOOK OF VOCATIONS

Not all the days in this set are celebrated every year. Those that are required should be chosen between New Year's Day and the Epiphany.

John the Baptist, Andrew and John, Simon Peter, Philip and Nathanael—Jesus' first disciples were given to him by the Baptist and they later brought others to him. but they were all called. "Come and see!" (Jn 1:39). "I saw you, Nathanael, under the fig tree" (1:48). Jesus and Nathanael look at each other, and other men too are so fascinated by him that they remain with him, the one to whom the Baptist pointed.

The first few pages of the fourth Gospel form a real "book of vocations," showing how deeply Jesus' call was felt. Staying, believing, bearing witness—each vocation is rooted in a deeply personal relationship with Christ. Paul claimed that he had been seized—made a "prisoner of Christ" (Eph 3:1). It is a faith that goes straight to the heart of revelation. John the Baptist was the first to bear witness: "He is the Chosen One of God" (Jn 1:34). And Jesus said to Nathanael: "You will see heaven laid open for the Son of Man" (1:51).

Heaven did open for those disciples, and the Father proclaimed that Jesus was his Son. They gave their faith to the one whom they recognized to be the Word of God, the Word calling for everything to be given up for his sake. They gave themselves to that Word, to Jesus who makes all things new and gathers all men together for the wedding feast of the eternal covenant. And from him they received a new name.

How could Christ's incarnation be good news for people of today if they no longer heard that voice and no longer encountered that glance? Christmas is not an illusion or a dream because it forms part of the flesh of our history and can therefore continue to be for us the dawn of a new world that God loved so much that he gave his only Son for it.

JANUARY 1

SOLEMNITY OF MARY, MOTHER OF GOD

The title "Mary, Mother of God" is reminiscent of the great theological debate that interested Christians of the first few centuries so deeply and even divided them. At the heart of that debate was the Trinitarian question. In other words, faith in the divinity of Jesus had to be reconciled with faith in the oneness of God. Many of the theologians of that time were content to make the Son subordinate to the Father. Some, like the bishop of Antioch, Paul of Samosata, went so far as to declare that Jesus was no more than a man in whom the word had dwelt "as in a temple." The champion of this tendency was undoubtedly Arius, who not only insisted that the Son was subordinate to the Father, but also refused to endow him with the nature and attributes of God, saying that he was not eternal, for example, and had not been divinely begotten. This Alexandrian priest, who was condemned by the First Council of Nicaea (325 A.D.), regarded the Word simply as a creature.

The Arians not only denied the divinity of the Son, they also diminished his humanity by refusing to accept that he had a human soul. They were in fact part of the gnostic movement in their devaluation of matter generally and of the humanity of Christ in particular—a doctrine which had already been refuted by the author of the First Epistle of John. Later, in the second century, Irenaeus of Lyons had developed a synthesis in which he demonstrated that Christ's work of redemption was derived from his recapitulation of all the phases of existence in total faithfulness to the Father. His synthesis was not, however, preserved as a whole and, although the unity of the person of Christ was generally admitted and presupposed as a point of departure, it was often explained in a one-sided manner. The West placed too much emphasis on reason, and the school of Alexandria stressed the aspect of revelation, insisting above all on the fact that Jesus, as the Word, enabled men to know the Father, but not giving a true value to his humanity.

The explanation that should have brought out the full significance of the Christological dogma led to a confrontation between the schools of Alexandria and Antioch in Syria. The Nicaean theology was admirably defended by the Alexandrian bishop Athanasius, who spent his whole life making the decisions of the Council known and accepted by the Church. He reintroduced the teaching of Irenaeus and especially the latter's theory of "exchange," according to which God became fully man so that man might also share in the divine life. He insisted on Jesus' divinity, but also taught that the human race would not have been authentically saved if Jesus had not assumed human nature in all its aspects. It is important, however, to note that Athanasius overlooked Jesus' human activity almost completely. He saw him as a being who was full of God, but purely passive, and this led to a reaction on the part of the school of Antioch, in which the authentic humanity of the Savior was stressed. Unlike the school of Alexandria, which emphasized the union of Christ's divine and human natures, Antioch insisted on their distinction and their fullness. The point of departure for the confrontation was provided by one of Athanasius' disciples, Apollinarius of Laodicea who, while claiming to be his master's spokesman, attacked the human nature of Christ. This evoked a violent response on the part of the Antiochian theologians Diodorus of Tarsus and Theodore of Mopsuestia. These rejected the incarnation as such and accepted only a mere indwelling of the Logos in the man Jesus. They did not believe in the birth of the Son of God, but only in the birth of a child in whom God dwelt.

The quarrel came to a head when a priest, Anastasius, criticized in his sermons the title "Mother of God" which had for a long time been given to Mary. Anastasius insisted that Mary could not be called Theotokos, but only Christotokos or "Mother of Christ." This affirmation gave rise to great indignation, because the title "Mother of God" enjoyed great favor among the people. Two parties emerged very rapidly. The first was led by Nestorius, who had been made bishop of Constantinople by the grace of the emperor, and the second by Cyril, the energetic bishop of Alexandria. The theological controversy also became political and sharpened the rivalry between the two most highly esteemed patriarchs of the Eastern Church. The Emperor Theodosius II summoned an ecumenical council at the instigation of Nestorius in 431 A.D. This Council of Ephesus was extremely stormy, and union was not achieved until 433 A.D., when the unity of the person of Christ was recognized as a truth of faith: "For of the two natures union is made. That is why we affirm one Christ, one Son, one Lord. Because of that union without confusion, we confess the holy Virgin, Mother of God."

∎

Nm 6:22–27: It has often been said that the title by which the Book of Numbers is know in Hebrew Bibles—"In the Desert"—perfectly describes the situation of Israel at the time. The book in fact deals with the formation of the people of God in the desert country bordering Palestine in the south and southeast.

The blessing contained in these verses has a very ancient form, but it must have been inserted into the collection at a later date. It seems to have been a blessing reserved for priests, although other documents show that kings also blessed their people. But all the underlying theology is priestly: Yahweh, who has no dwelling place on earth, nonetheless dwells in the midst of his people, thanks to the institution of priests and levites.

The verbs appear in the future in certain textual variants, thus giving a prophetic value to the blessing. This was moreover interpreted by some of the Church Fathers as a proclamation of the coming of Christ, "our peace and reconciliation."

Ps 67 is composite in its structure, combining prayer with a hymn. In it, the Lord is asked to show favor to his people.

Gal 4:4–7: In the previous chapter of the epistle, Paul has explained the part played by the law in the economy of salvation in revealing to man his weakness without being able to set him free. The law had not, however, canceled the promise made to Abraham. On the contrary, that promise had been fulfilled by the coming of Christ, whose incarnation inaugurated the time of fulfillment, which the apostle compares with the emancipation of a child.

Until then, the child possessed nothing in his own right. He could not claim possession of his goods and was subject to his guardians. His situation was comparable to that of a slave. Paul argues that both the Jews, who until the coming of Christ were subject to the law, and the pagans, who were subject to their passions, were in that situation. To set men free from this slavery, "God sent his Son, born of a woman, born a subject of the law." Jesus has, in other words, liberated men from their alienations in his concrete human existence.

Lk 2:16–21: There is a flavor of Easter in the story of the shepherds. Like the apostles in the Acts of the Apostles, they want to share the good news with everyone they meet and to celebrate the event by "glorifying and praising God for all they had heard and seen." The shepherds already belonged to the Church.

As in Acts too, Mary has her place in the missionary and praising Church. Like those who were entrusted with apocalyptic secrets, she "treasured and pondered in her heart" the events to which she had been the privileged witness. Their ultimate meaning would not, it is true, be revealed until Easter, but Mary had already praised the work of the Spirit in song when she visited her cousin Elizabeth. And the child in the manger—God saves—is, like Isaac, God's smile.

∎

You came in our flesh, Son of God,
  Son of Mary and our Brother.
  Enlighten our ways, Lord!

You are the Father's face
  and the sign of peace for the world.
  You are the mediator between God and men.
  Enlighten our ways, Lord!

You are the Word of renewal, the source of hope.
  Conceived by the Spirit, you are truly man.
  Enlighten our ways, Lord!

God of light,
  we bless you for every morning
  and for each new year—
  the promise of life and renewal.

God of tenderness,
  we bless you for each man's heart
  and for hands stretched out
  as a sign of peace.

God and Father of Jesus Christ,
  we bless you even more
  for the unfathomable reflection of your love

*that we see in your Son's eyes
when he looks at us.*

*We bless you and glorify you
for the one who embraced our flesh
and transfigures us in your light.*

*May your Church praise you
with the angels in heaven,
for you are the infinite God
and the God of tenderness.*

We acclaim you.

*Lord Jesus Christ,
your birth was the dawn of new peace
for those you love.
Look again at the love
that you have left in the heart of your Church
and, so that we may praise your glory
again in this new year,
join our hands together
in unity and joy.
Be with us, Emmanuel,
for a peace that will last
for ever and ever.*

JANUARY 2

HE CAME IN OUR FLESH
1 Jn 2:22–28: The child has grown up and has become a man. He has been tired. He has felt anger. He has been astonished. He has suffered and he died. Men have often been disturbed by Jesus' humanity and have preferred to stress his divinity and to reconstruct his life as a man

according to criteria that have seemed worthy of the Son of God. Attempts are always being made to transform his anger into "holy" anger.

It is precisely this error that is denounced in John's letter, which reminds believers of what they were "taught in the beginning" when they were being prepared for baptism. They were helped by the Spirit to accept that teaching. Those who believe do not in fact experience their faith as something that is outside themselves. On the contrary, the Word that they receive penetrates deeply into them like an anointing by the Spirit. They know and "do not need anyone to teach them." The author wrote these words when he was engaged in controversy with the gnostics, and it is difficult to know how the idea that faith is something within us could have been better expressed.

Ps 98 is a hymn inviting the whole earth to praise God. All the tenderness of God was reflected in the child in the crib.

Jn 1:19–28: "A voice cries: 'Prepare in the wilderness a way for Yahweh' " (Is 40:3). The theme of the new exodus, already present in Jeremiah and Ezekiel, is made explicit in Second Isaiah. The underlying principle was that the events that were to take place at the "end of time" would be a replica of the act of creation. Yahweh would "create new heavens and a new earth" and restore man to the first glory of Adam. Before this happened, however, Israel would take part in a new exodus, a kind of retreat in preparation for the promised land.

The prophet's words were interpreted in various ways by different people, John the Baptist, the members of the Qumran community and others, as an invitation to withdraw into the desert. John was aware of the imminence of the end of time and wanted above all to give the people a last chance to be radically converted to God. Yet, when he was questioned about his mission, he bore witness to another. He was not the Christ, nor was he Elijah, who, according to tradition, was to come back to exhort the people to repentance, nor the prophet of the end of time. His baptism was merely a water rite intended to set the seal on the inner conversion of his neophytes. The one whom everyone expected was, however, one of his disciples.

∎

"I am not the Messiah." It takes a great deal of insight into oneself to be able to say something like this. So many false messiahs and so many men who have raised and then disappointed people's hopes have arisen in every period of history that it is very tempting to call oneself a prophet, at least when one is sincere in one's ambitions and one's service of one's fellow men. How is it, then, that no one except Jesus Christ has been able to claim that he was the Messiah sent by God without trampling the very heart of Christian faith underfoot? What is that absolute quality that has been conferred on Jesus of Nazareth by orthodox believers and even by John the Baptist? This question is made all the more formidable by the fact that Jesus was and still is one of us—truly man. We give our faith, in other words, to a man whom we recognize to be "God-with-us."

The whole of the Gospel is a long road which we follow patiently, frequently stumbling, sometimes drawing back in doubt and sometimes with enthusiasm, gradually approaching that knowledge. We are at the heart of a paradox. God expresses himself in the humility of a man. Unlike all the demiurges, Jesus shows us a very humble face. And if he had been as brilliant as we sometimes depict him, why were his disciples so hesitant? Perhaps our idea of God had become dull.

We have therefore to recognize in Jesus the Son of the God whom no one has seen—the God who dwells beyond all light. The enigma of the Gospel will remain incomprehensible as long as we fail to understand the foolishness of God's love for his creation. It is because "God loved the world so much"—his world—"that he gave his only Son" (Jn 3:16). In him, God sees man and, in him, man also sees God. That is because there is, between God and man, a bond based on the extraordinary news that what is infinitely great is joined to what is infinitely small. The humility of man, taken from the earth, is the image and likeness of the glory of God.

We can, then, reply to all those who wrongly worship a Christ who is remote from our earth: the proof of the divinity of Jesus is that he was man to a degree that had and has never been reached before or since. But to appreciate that fully, we must withdraw into the desert, the only place where man can know that he is man.

■

You are not a remote God.
   You are called God-with-us.
We have touched your Son with our hands
   and have recognized in him
   the truth of our human hopes.
Lord God,
   keep us in the humility of faith
   and let us be in communion with you
   through your beloved Son, our Brother,
   Jesus, the Christ, our Lord.

You are greater than our hearts
   and you know everything.
   Lord, put your Spirit into us.

From the one who lives in love
   fear is for ever driven out.
   Lord, put your Spirit into us.

You loved us first
   and we have known your love.
   Lord, put your Spirit into us.
   (see 1 Jn 3:20; 4:18–19)

Unfathomable mystery of your love!
   You, God, living in infinity,
   came to dwell in our flesh.
Blessed are you for Jesus Christ,
   the first-born of your love,
   in whom we are your children.
We thank you for the words received from him
   as a promise of life:
   "Anyone who lives in love lives in God
   and God lives in him."
Yes, we believe in his words
   and with one heart
   we bless you.
   (see 1 Jn 4:16)

Our hands have received the bread of eternity
  and our lips have tasted the source of life.
Keep us, Lord, in faith and love,
  so that our communion with your Son
may also be communion with you
  the living God
  and source of all grace
  for ever and ever.

JANUARY 3

THE HOLY ONE OF GOD

1 Jn 2:29–3:6: In his second exposition (2:29–3:6), John defines in terms of sonship the communion that exists between God and man. He begins by stressing God's love and claiming that it makes the believer a child of God. Purified by the one who is without sin, our destiny is to become "as pure as Christ" (3:3), which is what we are intended to be.

The word "pure" has become devalued over the centuries and has therefore to be redefined, because the Christian's task to be "pure" has certain important consequences. The dictionary uses such words as "unmixed," "clear," "translucent" and so on to define it, but we might well ask: "Can man ever be pure, when he is a mixture of flesh and spirit?" The answer to this question can be found by contemplating the person of Christ. Could the Pure One of God only be pure outside the flesh, when he is the Word made flesh? And we can only understand the meaning of purity by looking at the Son of God until we become "like him"—in other words, by "seeing him as he really is." The world is not capable of doing this. God will always be hidden from the world, because it cannot see what is invisible through what is contingent and made of flesh.

Ps 98: see January 2.

Jn 1:29–34: Under the guidance of the Spirit, John the Baptist bears witness to Jesus: "I have seen and I am the witness that he is the Chosen

One of God." This testimony is indirectly addressed to some of the Baptist's own disciples who obstinately continued to regard him as the Messiah.

John also calls Jesus the "Lamb of God." This title seems to be the result of a post-paschal re-evaluation. In fact, if it is true that the Baptist saw in Jesus the one who was to restore Israel's purity, he would undoubtedly have used the title "Pure One of God," since Jesus is the one who makes pure anyone who believes in him. The author of the fourth Gospel, however, would seem to have reinterpreted the title in the light of the Easter event: Jesus took away the sin of the world in offering himself on the cross. He handed himself over to men, just as the lamb presents his sides to the one who shears him. And did he not die at the very time when the heads of families sacrificed the paschal lamb in the forecourt of the temple (see 1 Cor 5:7b)?

■

How dangerous words become when they are devalued! And yet an extraordinary symphony of words can be heard within us today in praise of God's love and faithfulness. But what sound do we hear when we listen to the apostle's words: "Surely everyone who entertains this hope must purify himself, must try to be as pure as Christ"? Purity! At once, as soon as we hear that word, the horizon narrows down, overshadowed by centuries of agonizing. And yet, does not purity mean, quite simply, "what is unmixed, clear and translucent"? And then we hesitate again, since we think of the union of body and spirit in man as a mixture that is far from clear. And what about Jesus Christ? Can he, the Pure One, the Holy One of God, be pure outside the flesh? He is, after all, the Word made flesh. We can, as we have seen, only really comprehend purity by contemplating the Son of God until we become "like him" by "seeing him as he really is."

Just consider how important "seeing" is in the language of Christian revelation. The Baptist, for example, says: "I saw the Spirit coming down on him," and the apostle says, in his First Letter: "We shall be like him because we shall see him as he really is." And then we are reminded of the Beatitude: "Happy are the pure in heart: they shall see God" (Mt 5:8).

Purity and seeing are interdependent. "Because the world refused to acknowledge God, it does not acknowledge us." God is always concealed from the eyes of the world, which cannot see the invisible God through the flesh. The Baptist points to Jesus because he is able to see, but what he sees is not in any way an extraordinary phenomenon. It is a very simple reality contemplated in its deep unity. John was quite pure, and he saw the manifestation of the Spirit where others saw nothing. It is possible that faith today has come to grips with the same need.

We are children of God and Jesus is the Son of God. The ultimate reality, which is only revealed through its translucence, is always pointing in the direction of being, not of morality. Jesus is not the Son of God as the consequence of having behaved in an exemplary fashion. He is God's Son because of his incarnation. He is at the very root of his being the Son of God. And we are children of God in the same way. The Spirit can be seen as the agent of that existence. John saw the Spirit "rest" on Jesus, who was "going to baptize with the Holy Spirit"—in other words, immerse us and enable us to be born in the Spirit, making us sons of God. But what is sonship if it is not a relationship of love? Man is father (mother) and continues to be father (or mother) by being in a relationship of love with another. That is above all so in the case of God the Trinity and God-with-us. The "love that the Father has lavished on us" is not just a special favor, something given on the side. We are not simply "called" to be children of God. We *are* children of God. The love of God the Trinity, of whom the Spirit is the heart, makes us his children. Not only Jesus' humanity, but also our own is transfigured in God by the creative grace of Love. But that relationship comes to us through the Son, to whom the Father has given all power. And above all he has power to give life to those who believe in him.

"Surely everyone who entertains this hope must purify himself, must try to be as pure as Christ." And the true name of purity is, of course, love. Love, after all, is unmixed, clear and translucent. Love can enable us to see what is invisible. It is without fear (1 Jn 4:18). It knows God. What must the Baptist's love of Jesus have been? Infinite purity which could not stifle those longings that are expressed in the very approximate language of human love.

John saw the Spirit come down like a dove. So many symbols are expressed in this, and they are unmixed. The dove of glowing purity. The white dove, with a whiteness evoking the holiness of God. The dove of peace, carrying the branch to the ark of the new world and proclaiming a world of the love of sons. The Spirit hovering over the world on that first morning, giving it the warmth of life. The Spirit raising to life the Lamb of God on the morning of that day without end. Happy are the hearts that can contemplate these things unceasingly. For them, everything is pure.

∎

Blessed are you, God our Father.
  You call us your children.
  You beget us every day
  in Jesus, your Son.
We ask you:
  Pour out your Spirit into us,
  so that, every day,
  we can call you Father,
  for ever and ever.

Open our eyes, Lord,
in the translucence of your light.
May we never cease to contemplate
Jesus your son who came in our flesh,
until the day when we become like him
by seeing him face to face
as he really is, for ever and ever.

JANUARY 4

FASCINATION
1 Jn 3:7–10: The style of 1 John can easily confuse the reader who is unfamiliar with the parallelisms of the Hebrew language. It is important to be aware of them in this text. In 3:4, for example, the author writes:

"Anyone who commits sin at all breaks the law," which, translated more literally, reads as: "Anyone doing sin also does iniquity," where the parallelism is clear. In 3:8, there is another parallel: "To lead a sinful life (= the one doing sin) is to belong to the devil (= is of the devil)." It is important, then, to define the term "iniquity." It is used in fact by the author to describe the incredulity of the Jews who failed to recognize Jesus during his lifetime and of the gnostics who, at the time that the letter was written, rejected the incarnation of the son of God.

There are other antitheses in this text. The first text mentioned above, 3:4, can, for example, be contrasted with 3:7b: "To live a holy life is to be holy," which is more literally rendered as "the one doing righteousness is righteous," a version that clearly goes back to an antithesis between "iniquity" or "unrighteousness" and "justice" or "righteousness" as the quality that characterizes the man who keeps to the divine covenant. "Righteousness" here can be understood in the sense of "doing the truth," an attitude that is made possible by the presence in the believer of the "seed," which is, according to both St. Augustine and Luther, the word of God.

John also says that "no one who has been begotten by God sins." This statement testifies to the author's conviction that God's word is extremely powerful in man. In the Old Testament, the power enabling men to triumph over sin comes from the law, the word of God, existing within the hearts of the righteous. The prophets believed that man's purification by the inner law characterized the messianic period. In verse 10, the same idea recurs in a statement by the author that the practice of righteousness presupposes a communion of brothers that is also "incarnate." He states this negatively: "anyone not loving his brother is no child of God."

Ps 98: see January 2.

Jn 1:35–42: After having been baptized, Jesus formed part of the Baptist's group of disciples, walking "behind" John and baptizing as well. There can be little doubt, however, that he quite soon achieved seniority among his companions, with the result that the Baptist's movement had two leaders. But John, the "bridegroom's friend" (3:29), knew that Jesus was the "Lamb of God" (1:29) and that his mission had been fulfilled. So, like the old man Simeon, he rejoiced.

John's disciples joined Jesus. They were all Galileans. Andrew, Simon and Philip were from Bethsaida. Nathanael was a scribe, and Jesus had seen him meditating "under the fig tree" (1:48), that is, according to the rabbinic tradition, "under the tree of the knowlege of good and evil." Jesus had been a disciple of John's and his companions were from Galilee. The beginning of his ministry was essentially human. It was also part of the incarnation.

■

If we look carefully, we can see the power of God at work in everything that Jesus does and says. That power has great fascination. During his lifetime, it attracted men to him. They felt a fresh wind blowing in their hearts. His glance alone was irresistibly fascinating. He looked at the first disciples, his glance penetrated into their hearts, and they responded and followed him immediately. Only one thing mattered in the call that they heard—that God was fascinating and was able to lead them further and further.

Woe to the man who has never been struck by lightning. He may think that he is living, but he is really only vegetating. His days pass, already weighed down by the weight of death. Happy is the man who has been fascinated and attracted. He is guided by burning love and wakes up every morning ready to set off again on an endless journey in search of the treasure for which he has given up everything.

Woe to the man whose faith is closed and sheltered. He may sleep in peace, but will be too late when he wakes up. His heart will be too hardened to hear the voice calling him. Happy is the disciple who is fascinated by Jesus Christ—the man in whom Jesus lives. He is listening and watching night and day and his heart is passionately alive.

It would be wonderful to know what Jesus said during that day to the two disciples who had been so fascinated by his glance. But it is always indiscreet to record the mere words spoken in a loving conversation. Yet I think I know what he said to them. It was just one word—the word that lived in his Son's heart. He told them—or should we say that they saw in his glance?—that God is love, that God is everything, and that we must leave everything when he calls.

Happy is the Christian who never ceases to look at Jesus Christ. He will be fascinated by him. And, whatever happens, he will return again and again to his first love, because Christ's glance is the infinitely loving glance of God for man and for all men. Do you remember the last conversation that Peter had with Jesus, after that impossible night when the disciple thought he could go back to his nets? "Simon, son of John, do you love me?" "Yes, Lord, you know I love you . . . . You know everything; you know I love you" (Jn 21:15–17). There is nothing else to say when one has been "begotten by God." The man who has been begotten by God cannot sin—he has set off on the road of love.

■

Lord Jesus, beloved Son of the Father,
   you offered your life for us
   as an incalculable treasure.
Let us share the delight of the true disciple
   and joyfully leave everything
   to follow you
   for ever and ever.

For those who have followed you and who dwell in you
   and for those who resist your call,
   God, knowing that you want man's good, we pray.

For those who love in the freedom of the Spirit
   and for those who are afraid to give themselves to others,
   God, knowing that you reveal yourself in love, we pray.

For your Church, knowing that you want us to be poor and to serve,
   and for those who distort your Gospel,
   God, manifested in humility, we pray.

Lord Jesus, you are light.
   Whoever receives you
   will discover the ways of life.
Come and dispel our darkness,
   so that our hands, held out to welcome you,
   may also be joined in a sign of peace
   and a token of unity and life.

We have followed you, Lord,
   and you have remained with us.
We have recognized you at this table—
   you are the bread of life.
When we have to set off again on our way,
   let us remain with our brothers
   and be for them
   the bread of hope
   and the word of the future.
Make us your disciples
   until we take our place
   at your table
   in the eternal kingdom.

JANUARY 5

OPEN-HEARTED LOVE
1 Jn 3:11–21: At the beginning of his exposition, John noted that the world could never know the cost of love because it did not know what love was. He returns to this theme here, calling the world the place of hatred. The believer, however, has the example of Jesus before him—the one who "gave up his life for us."

God, then, was so committed to loving men that he embraced the cross. We have therefore to respond by loving without reservation. Heavenly love was made incarnate in the glance of Jesus Christ. Our love must be made concrete in the way we look at our fellow men. We must not look, as Cain did, with envy and hatred. No—our glance must be gentle and understanding. In that way we shall be able to live in peace. Even if our hearts accuse us, we shall still be at peace, knowing that God is greater than our hearts.

Ps 100 is a hymn inviting believers to praise God's love for his people in song.

Jn 1:43–51: John ends this chapter on bearing witness with Jesus' words: "You will see heaven laid open and, above the Son of Man, the angels of God ascending and descending." These words are reminiscent of Jacob-Israel's dream (Gn 28:10–19) in which the patriarch had a vision of a ladder placed between heaven and earth. This dream referred to the founding of the sanctuary of Bethel. According to the legend, the local god had appeared in a dream to a distant ancestor, who had seen him descending what seem to have been the ramps of a ziggurat. It was possible in this way to account for the function of the temple, which was to be the place where heaven and earth met, the gate of heaven and the house of God.

When he spoke these words, then, Jesus was proclaiming the fact that he was the gate of heaven. Certain rabbis interpreted this dream in the following way: "The angels jumped and leaped on Israel to strengthen him, for it is said of Israel that he is the one in whom I shall be glorified." In this way, they linked the patriarch's vision to the songs of the suffering servant (Is 42). But John makes a very interesting comparison when he puts the figure of the Son of Man in the place of Israel, since, like the suffering servant, "the Son of Man has been glorified and God has been glorified in him" (Jn 13:31). By dying on the cross, Jesus fulfilled the mission given to the servant to bring Israel together again and bring light to the nations. From that time onward, a bridge had been built between man and God.

Jesus' reply to Nathanael ends the chapter on bearing witness and opens the "Book of Signs" which will illustrate the vision of new heavens.

■

Nathanael—a loyal man and an exemplary scribe. Sitting under his fig tree, he examines in detail and with great care both good and evil. He is not really open to unexpected encounters. His ideas are preconceived. But he is incapable of lying. There are many religious men like him. But at least he trusts Philip.

And once again we have those glances, that looking and seeing. "I saw you," Jesus says to the scribe, who is at once overcome by Jesus' power of attraction. But that first manifestation is only a beginning and Nathanael must go further. "You will see greater things than that." You will see what can only be seen by faith. You used to examine the words of Scripture as though it was a closed network, but now you will see that heaven is open and you will discover the unexpected truth. "You are the Son of God," you replied, perhaps too quickly, but you will see in him whom you answered a Son of Man whom God will raise up despite death. You were a scribe, Nathanael, but from now on you will bear witness to love.

Our lives are like that. We examine good and evil because we want to define the outlines of love and know the demands that it makes and the direction in which it is going. Like Nathanael, we are honest and upright, yet our hearts are cramped, and sooner or later they accuse us (see 1 Jn 3:19–20). We want to experience love, but we do not really want to be given life from its source and so we hardly dare to stand up confidently in God's presence. We have to wait, then, for the day when someone looks at us and says: "I know you." And he knows us with his heart and takes us further, to the point where we see the source and everything is possible, because everything is bathed in God.

It is not enough simply to love. We have to love in the thrust of God's love. What, then, is that astonishing vision that we are promised? Surely it is a vision of God-Love, who begets his Son and gives us his Spirit. The one who has seen the source looks no further—he only wants to love open-heartedly. He is quite confident. His heart is still all too human, but he is no longer hesitant. He has passed from death to life. He is at peace and bears witness to another world. He no longer examines good and evil, but lets the life-giving water from the source flow through him "beyond good and evil." Those words are blasphemous only when applied to those who have never been conscious of the Son of Man looking at them with his fiery glance— the Son of Man who died for love and was raised again by Love. If only you had known, Nathanael!

JANUARY 6

HEAVEN IS OPEN
1 Jn 5:5–13 and Ps 147: see the Friday after Epiphany.

Mk 1:7–11: "My testimony is greater than John's . . . . The Father who sent me bears witness to me himself" (Jn 5:36–37). During the age of the patriarchs, all the righteous benefited from the Spirit of God, but after the people had sinned by worshiping the golden calf, Yahweh limited the gift of the Spirit to the kings, prophets and priests of Israel. The Spirit was completely extinguished when the last prophet died.

Here Jesus comes to John and asks him for baptism. When he emerges from the river, the heavens are torn apart like a piece of old material, and the dove of the flood proclaims to the whole world that this man is filled with the Holy Spirit. Once again God's voice is heard, saying that Jesus is his Chosen One and his beloved Son.

∎

For forty days the rain fell. There was a terrible flood. Heaven was closed and God's sun no longer shone on the world of men. The night was endless, a darkness in which all life was extinguished, swallowed up by the storm. Only Noah, carried by the raft of hope, expected God to remember.

Forty days—a testing time. When that time had passed, Noah released the raven, the bearer of death. The raven was comfortable with him, finding food without even looking for it. Then Noah sent out the dove, the bird that flies up toward life and reflects the glory of heaven. It took the dove seven days, the time taken for creation, to encounter life and return bearing a green olive branch. Then seven more days passed and the dove did not come back, because life had begun again in a new world. Since that time, the dove has come to symbolize life and hope.

For forty days Jesus was in the desert, the country of death. For forty days he was put to the test. His life was, as it were, foreshortened. But he went into the desert to sow life there, because God

remembered in him and heaven opened in him. I will never again lay the earth waste, God said.

Jesus carries life in himself, and the dove comes down on him and rests on him. Hope is there at that meeting. The breath of wind that had set the earth free to recreate it has become the Breath of God, Spirit and Life. Like a dove, the messenger of a new world, the Spirit descends on the Messiah and rests on him. He is to plant an olive tree in the desert.

Heaven is open. The rainbow of light is shining in the sky. The sign of the covenant bathes in light the one who is God's covenant with men. Never again will life be overcome by a flood. Death will rush forward to attack the one sent by God, and he will be swallowed up in the tomb, but God will remember and raise his Son up on the morning of the new day—on that eighth day when the week that has no end begins. An eternal covenant binds God to our earth. The rainbow is the sign of that covenant—a circle of light enclosing the earth—and the promise of resurrection and hope.

■

You are always greater than our plans
 and your plan goes far beyond our expectations.
You begot your Son in the Spirit.
Immerse us, Lord,
 in the ocean of your love;
 make our horizons as wide as yours
 and renew us, your children, in the Spirit,
 so that, in Jesus, we may live from you
 for ever and ever.

JANUARY 7

WINE AT THE WEDDING
1 Jn 5:14–21 and Ps 150: see the Saturday after Epiphany.

Jn 2:1–12: Numbers are important here. "Three days later there was a wedding at Cana in Galilee." This "third day" is more than just an indication of the chronology. The event at Cana took place three days after Jesus' promise to Nathanael that he would see "heaven laid open" (Jn 1:51). And, like the Book of Genesis, the fourth Gospel opens with a week ending, on the seventh day, with a first manifestation of salvation in favor of man.

So it was a village wedding. Six jars had been set up in a courtyard for the ritual ablutions—six hundred liters of water so that the law of purity could be observed. But God comes to the wedding. There is no more need for water in those jars. That can only cleanse man externally. Now it is his heart that is going to be renewed. Be joyful, Church, because today your God is going to marry you. Today is the banquet of the covenant and the wine will flow—six hundred liters of the best vintage: a unique occasion.

It is Jesus' first manifestation. There will be others, and they will all express the tenderness of God. The last sign will be the cross raised between earth and heaven when the hour has come. Then the new wine will be poured into the cup of the covenant, the blood and water will flow from the side of the crucified Christ, and Mary will be at the foot of the cross.

■

There was dancing and singing. But in their happiness the guests drank deeply and the reserves of wine ran out. Mary, who was conscious of everything, saw the host frowning sadly, thinking that the guests would call him stingy.

Is there ever enough wine when the spirits of the wedding guests are dancing and singing? Is it possible to ration love when people wake up to a new day bathed in the sun of life? The Spirit cannot be crushed when the Church drinks at the very source of life. "The days are coming . . . when the mountains will run with new wine and the hills all flow with it" (Am 9:13). We are drunk with love when wine gladdens our hearts. And it is very sad when our hearts are closed and we prefer the water of the law to the freedom of the Spirit. On the day of Pentecost, some people who were indifferent laughed and said: "They have been drinking too much new wine" (Acts 2:13). Who can ever understand the Spirit?

"Woman, why turn to me?" Yes, I have come so that your heart will tremble with happiness. You have preferred me and you will never again be called "wilderness." Yes, woman, the Spirit will make you drunk and his freedom will make you fertile, but "my hour has not yet come." And yet, for you, from now on I will manifest my glory and my love. What does it matter when the Spirit blows and nobody knows where it comes from and where it goes (see Jn 3:8)?

Love is overflowing. The Spirit gives without counting how much. Today six hundred liters of wine—tomorrow blood given to the last drop. The hour is approaching. Today the wedding has begun—tomorrow love will give its fruit. When the hour did come, he loved them to the end. The Spirit was poured out from his wounded heart so that the cup of wine in our hands would be the sign of the covenant.

"They have been drinking too much new wine." He was the first—the Bridegroom who gives his blood. He longed to drink the cup with them. At Cana he could not resist the Spirit and he agreed to give everything for the sake of the woman who carried in herself his brothers and sisters. Bride and mother, the woman at his side—he obeyed her, until the time came for him to take her to the wine-press of the cross where love would be fulfilled.

■

You invite us to the feast
  and arrange a meeting for the wedding.
Lord, fill us with your Spirit
  and let our cup overflow with new wine.
Let our lives be the song of the new covenant
  for ever and ever.

THE WEEK AFTER THE EPIPHANY:
THE MANIFESTATIONS OF THE WORD

We have trivialized the Epiphany and turned it into a feast of kings or a story of magicians or astrologers. We have forgotten that it is above all the feast of the manifestation. Our Christian brothers in the East celebrate it with a solemnity that expresses the great mystery of faith much better. The Epiphany is also simultaneously a celebration of the coming of the magi, the baptism of the Lord and the wedding at Cana. According to a very old antiphon, still preserved in the Liturgy of the Hours, "Today the Church has been joined to her heavenly Bridegroom, since Christ has purified her of her sins in the river Jordan; the magi hasten to the royal wedding and offer gifts and the wedding guests rejoice since Christ has changed water into wine."

The theme of the manifestations of the Incarnate Word is extended in the Gospels throughout this week. We listen to the word spoken by Jesus at Nazareth and Capernaum, we observe his acts of goodness, multiplying the loaves or healing a leper, and we witness signs of his power (his walking on the water). In all these manifestations, he is the Bridegroom who comes to save men and lead them to life. He reveals God and manifests the Father's love.

In place of fear he puts peace. To those who walk in darkness he brings light. To the man who loves he says: You know God. To the one who listens to his words he says: Today it is fulfilled for you. The manifestation of God in Jesus Christ is not just an old story. It is the task of the liturgy to make that manifestation present every day by thanking God who calls us every day, asking us to come to him in love and faith.

MONDAY AFTER THE EPIPHANY

LIGHT AT THE CROSSROADS
1 Jn 3:22–4:6: One consequence of the inner law that fills the believer with life now is that he cannot ask for anything that will not be in accordance with God's will. God's commandment is perfectly fulfilled in his confession of Jesus Christ as the Son of God and in his life of brotherly love. If he keeps this commandment, he can be sure that "God lives in him."

At the end of this second exposition, the apostle, very conscious of the crisis that is dividing the churches, returns to the question of the criterion of faith: "You can tell the Spirit of God by this: every spirit which acknowledges that Jesus Christ has come in the flesh is from God, but any spirit which will not say this of Jesus is not from God." Finally, he insists that the word of God is mediated by men and that means, under the present circumstances, the preaching of the apostles. Whoever believes in the apostolic preaching is open to a knowledge of God, and those who have been strengthened by this in their adherence to the truth of the Church's faith will certainly "overcome the false prophets."

Ps 2: A revolt against the king! In the ancient world, a change of monarch was often the signal for a revolt against the dynasty in power. Here the king has the best of all reasons to be confident—Yahweh himself has given him his throne and is governing his destiny. This psalm was given a Christological interpretation in the early Church, the cross of Christ being seen as the sign of contradiction in the heart of every Christian.

Mt 4:12–17, 23–25: After the death of Solomon, the land of Israel was divided by schism. The northern provinces proclaimed their independence while the south of the country remained faithful to the crown in Jerusalem. This division scandalized Jewish patriots, many of whom looked forward to a Messiah who would restore the nation's unity. But in 732 B.C. the north of Galilee was annexed by the Assyrian army and the division of the country seemed to be complete and final. Even the provinces seemed to have different destinies.

Now, however, a man appears in Capernaum and proclaims the coming of the kingdom and the urgent need for conversion. Men experience a resurgence of hope. Will the old curse be removed? On the "land of deep shadow a light has shone" (Is 8:23b–9:1). At Capernaum, Jesus speaks to the "Galilee of the nations" and he also goes to other places, such as Sepphoris and Tiberias, where there is a large Greek population, sometimes in a majority. The kingdom of God is certainly coming closer in the person of Jesus, who takes on himself the sicknesses and infirmities of his fellow men. Indeed, those who are in suffering come from Galilee, the Decapolis, Jerusalem and the whole of Judea. He even becomes well known among the Syrians. A new era is dawning.

■

Jesus goes back to Galilee. His life with John the Baptist has come to an end, and from now on he will be a wandering prophet—God's nomad, looking for those who are lost. And he begins this new life at the crossroads with the pagans—his brothers. He is, like his disciples, a Galilean, and he will not be forgotten in Jerusalem. But he knows that God's ways are not parallel with those of men. So he begins his mission by bringing light to the crossroads of a world divided between the traditional religion of the ancestors and the attraction from outside. He begins, in other words, in "Galilee of the nations." For Christ, that world calls to mind that time long ago when God brought his enslaved people back by the sea road that runs by Galilee, the time when he broke the yoke of the captives and made the great cry for freedom and return break out. Now Jesus himself goes back to the country that bears the sign of slavery and darkness—a country with a bad reputation. He is going to speak to the people of peace, joy and real freedom. So his first words are: "Repent!"

Repent—be converted! Familiar words, but so often misused or misunderstood! When we hear them, we think of our wretched habits, of every conversion being followed by a falling back into past errors and our being imprisoned in our own darkness. But surely Jesus means something different. A business that is so weighed down with debts and antiquated machinery or methods has to be converted into something new if it is to succeed, and that is what Jesus is suggesting—a new way along which we can look for a new world. So again and again he says: "Follow me!"

The whole of the Gospel presupposes a way, a road, walking, learning, discovering a new horizon every morning and a real "today"

every day. It hardly matters who we are. The fishermen of Galilee had hands hardened by work. They were full of enthusiasm, but not very steadfast. And they had everything to learn. "Repent!" If there is a kingdom, you have to set off on the road followed by your fellow men and proclaim it to them. The rest is not important. When day breaks on a new morning, you have to put the night behind you and think no more about the darkness of your past. Be converted! At each crossroad you have to appeal to everyone who is looking for the light. Then your task is to lead all those people to the source of life. We all have to be converted, changed, simply and radically into people with faith in Jesus Christ who love each other as he has commanded us.

TUESDAY AFTER THE EPIPHANY

LOVING IS KNOWING

1 Jn 4:7–10: In his third and final exposition, John returns to the criteria of communion with God. In the two previous expositions, he provided three of these criteria—one negative, the abandonment of sin, and two positive, charity and faith. In this exposition, he does not mention the first criterion, but deals only with the other two, which he traces back to their source. On the one hand, he shows that love comes from God and is rooted in faith (4:7–21) and, on the other, he argues that faith in the Son of God is also at the root of charity (5:1–12). There is also a close parallelism between the beginning of this exposition and the end of the second one. In 4:2, the author says: "Every spirit which acknowledges that Jesus the Christ has come in the flesh is from God." In 4:7, he says: "Everyone who loves is begotten by God and knows God."

"Everyone who loves . . . knows God." Here we are at the level of biblical "knowledge." This knowledge is composed of close intimate complicity and inner sharing. The definition of the Christian is in fact very close to that of God himself. Everyone who practices love, John is saying, experiences love, "because God is love." His definition is in no sense abstract. This is clear from his insistence on what the history of salvation has to teach us. God initiated the process by "sending into the world his only Son, so that we could have life through him." Then he initiated the process of love. The most convincing proof of all is that "he loved us first" (1 Jn 4:19). John's argument is a long way from the superior, knowing and intellectual illumination of the gnostics.

"God, give your own justice to the king, your own righteousness to the royal son." Ps 72 lists the qualities that Israel expected the king to have and provide: peace, security on the frontiers, bread and above all a refuge from unjust judges. This psalm was, of course, applied to the king in the messianic age.

Mk 6:34–44: What have they done to my people, the shepherds of Israel? They have abandoned their sheep, so that they have become scattered and the prey of wild beasts. They have strayed all over the country and "no one bothers about them and no one looks for them." The prophet Ezekiel condemned the free and easy laxity of the Jewish leaders by comparing them to bad shepherds (Ez 34). At the same time, however, he proclaimed that Yahweh would "raise up one shepherd" who would "pasture his sheep and be their shepherd" (34:23).

What are those in charge of the people doing now? They should take the Church back to the desert and let it sit down at the table of the word and the bread. The people of God would sit down, as they did at the time of Moses in the desert, "in squares of hundreds and fifties" and God would fascinate them by speaking to their hearts.

In the desert of the world, the Church will drink at the source of life. Jesus will take bread, pronounce a blessing and break it, so that it can be distributed among the people. The future age will break into our world and establish a bridgehead with that world where "there will be no more mourning or sadness" (Rv 21:4).

■

How are we to define love? According to the dictionary, it is, for example, a lively affection, a passionate feeling and so on. There is always some irrational element in love, something that cannot be programmed. It is a mode of being that is opposed to the cold reason that tries to account for and establish logical minimums and possible compromises. Love comes from the heart. It is overflowing. It begins where reason ends. I think that our contemporary lack of faith is very similar to the crisis in love that has existed for a very

long time in the Western world. We are stretched out between what Kant called "religion within the limits of reason" and the excesses of passion, and we have no aim and no guide. But these two extremes can be reconciled in faith because God is love, an endless and overflowing source. Love is a gift of self, without limits, a joy that is so full that it goes beyond all selfishness. We Christians believe in love. Our faith is simply faith in love.

"Everyone who loves . . . knows God." The word "know" is extremely important. It means, for example, "being born with" or "becoming one with." Love is the very place of knowledge. All our experience of love bears witness to this. We can only know the other person if we hand ourselves over to him and let him hand himself over to us. Very few people really know each other, because most people hold themselves in reserve, are closed in on themselves, do not venture to trust the other or entrust the secret of their heart to the other and are afraid to let their interchange with the other come from the root, as Newman said.

But God initiates this knowledge. He knows us first because he ties himself to us, entrusts the root of his being to us and calls us to come to him so that we may become one with him. God has known us since the day that he was born-with-us, creating us with his innermost breath. From every point of view it is true that love is tied to breath. Our heart begins to leap, and that is God moving in us. "Everyone who loves . . . knows God." He experiences God-in-him and that is an endless experience, because no one can ever have enough of it. When we see with the eyes of faith, knowledge of God is always beyond reason, at the level of the heart, in the ecstasy of charity. It is there that we know the God who is not closed solitude, but infinite life.

The multiplication of the loaves in the desert is the sign and the sacrament of that experience. The bread is shared infinitely because it is the bread of love. It is the bread of Christ's sorrow for the people who have been abandoned. He loves them, more than he is required to by reason, and he does not want to send them away hungry. He will, after all, be for them the "good shepherd who lays down his life for his sheep" (Jn 10:11). In Jesus Christ we have known God's love for us.

Someone who loves is as good as bread for others. Do we ever think about that when we share the Eucharist with others? The Eucharist is the place where we can know God, but not by eating the body of the Lord in isolation, each one of us gathering strength for himself alone. No, we know God in the Eucharist insofar as the table of Christ becomes an experience of the love of God revealed in his Son who is as good as bread for us and for others and who became bread shared infinitely for all men.

∎

God, whom no eye has ever seen,
   you give yourself to be known
   in the glance of love.
You, living so far beyond us,
   speak in hearts that are full of charity.
Stay with us, so that we may dwell in you.
   Open our eyes, so that we become aware of your presence.
   Increase our love,
   so that we may know the joy of knowing you
   in the charity that unites us
   today and every day
   for ever and ever.

You loved us to the end—
   God of love, forgive us.
So that we may love our brothers in truth—
   God of love, be with us.

So that we may know you as you know us—
   God of love, stay with us.

Lord Jesus,
   only Son,
   full of grace and truth—
will our eyes one day see
   your glory?
You already reveal yourself to us
   in the sacrament of shared bread

and the splendor of your love
   is already expressed in the humility of our acts.
Let us continue to be astonished,
   and may your Eucharist always be
   the foretaste and the token
   of the face to face
   when we shall know you
   in the full light of your glory.

WEDNESDAY AFTER THE EPIPHANY

BEYOND FEAR

1 Jn 4:11–18: "Since God has loved us so much, we too should love one another." That is the basis of love. It has its source in God. God is its model. Man's love shares in God's love of man: "We are to love, then, because he loved us first." This takes us back to the first days of the world's existence, when man was created in the image and likeness of God. All the love that man can contain has its source in God, and that fullness of love was made manifest when God "sent his Son to be the sacrifice that takes our sins away" (4:10). Faith is in this way closely linked to love. The apostle expresses this thought in the following concise way: "We have known and put our faith in God's love towards ourselves."

The question of criteria for our communion with God is raised again in verse 12: "No one has ever seen God." How, then, can we be sure that we are in communion with him? We have already seen that faith in Jesus Christ as the incarnate Son is a guarantee of this. Now John also points to charity: "As long as we love one another, God will live in us and his love will be complete in us." But the apostle does not want us to think of God or love in abstract terms. Our love must be fully "incarnate": "Anyone who says 'I love God' and hates his brother is a liar" (4:20). In fact, faith and love of the brothers are a sharing in the Spirit of God and that Spirit is at the source of the testimony of the apostles and at the same time of the hope of the believer when he is confronted with the last judgment: "In love there can be no fear."

Ps 72: see the Tuesday after Epiphany.

Mk 6:45–52: Who is this Jesus who has fed his people? The disciples get into their boat, but he seeks solitude and prayer. It is getting dark and the fishermen are afraid. It is dangerous on the lake. Who knows—Leviathan, that monster from another age, may attack them. What could hardened hearts do if the forces of evil were unleashed?

Who is this Jesus who has fed his people? They see him now emerging from the dark background of the night and trampling the water of the lake underfoot. Who is Jesus? He is the God of the exodus, the God of Moses.

He has been praying on the mountain and now he is coming back to his own. He has seen the glory of the Father and he will reveal it now to the Twelve. But before they can see it, their hearts must open and they must die to themselves. Then, in the humble sign of the cross, they will know the glory of God.

■

"Do not be afraid." The disciples' relationship with Jesus is not yet one of love, trust and openness to the mystery. They think he is a ghost. Their minds are full of the terrors that haunt men who have not yet encountered God face to face in a passionate but serene meeting. They still do not know what is happening because they have not yet penetrated into the heart of the Lord and the intensity of the love that comes from God. Their hearts are closed. They are turned in on themselves. They are blind. They are afraid.

"Fear is driven out by perfect love." Anyone who remains in fear has not reached the perfection of love. Let's be honest. How many anxieties and even neuroses are caused by religious feelings of the wrong kind! We are afraid of God because we have gone off in search of him weighed down with prohibitions, ill at ease and looking for a security that does not exist, when we should simply have opened our hearts. We still insist on talking about a threatening God who follows and punishes us. Our hearts can only be healed if we associate with Jesus for a long time and trust completely in the freedom of love.

Associate with Jesus! Look at him getting into the boat with his disciples! He sits down among them and the wind drops. Nothing very special, but he is present and their anxiety and fear are dispelled. They become calm. Who is he, then? His identity is made clear in the course of one encounter after another, when his glance brings peace and serenity. In him, God's love has the face of friendship, benevolence and freedom.

Trust in love! Look at Jesus walking on the waves. He does it freely and quite easily. It is a good image, but unfortunately it reminds us too of those warnings that we give to children—and to grown-up children—who spend their lives dealing quite easily with dangers that they do not seem to notice. Don't do this! Don't do that! God, how annoying fear is when you rely on love! And how much I enjoy walking on the water! "In love there can be no fear."

As we all know, love can at times be stormy as the waters of a lake in a high wind and as dangerous as the gusts driving the threatened boat. But what does it matter? "I fear no harm; beside me your rod and your staff are there to hearten me" (Ps 23:4). Everything depends on our continuing, whatever happens, to "live in love": "Anyone who lives in love lives in God and God lives in him." We may have to swallow a few bitter pills and we may make a few mistakes, but we must go on living in that love, in which "there can be no fear." We have to acquire a different way of life and a different way of knowing God—the only way that will not give rise to the worst form of all human neuroses, religious anxiety.

Love, then, and, as St. Augustine said, do what you will. But do not look away from Christ, and, as often as you can, join him on the mountain and pray with him. then you will learn how to love more and more and to do more and more what you will.

■

When we are gripped by fear,
   come to us, Lord, and sit beside us.
   Make us live with you.
When we are anxious,
   give us a brother to love
   and fill our hearts with the passion of love.
May your Spirit open in us
   the door to adventure.
   There is no peace without the freedom
   which you invite us to share,
   so that we may live with you

without fear or anxiety
and as freely as at the end of time.

Stay with us, Lord Jesus,
  so that we may live in you.

Live in our poverty,
  so that we may know your grace.

Enlighten our darkness,
  so that we may walk in the light.

Reveal your truth to us,
  so that we may bear witness to your love.

Blessed are you, Lord Emmanuel,
  God of men,
  for endless ages.

Jesus, you are the shepherd
  who brings back those who have gone astray
  and you give us your body as food.
Blessed are you
  for that blessing that will never cease.
We pray
  that your presence will produce in us
  the fruits of unity and peace
  in the service of our brothers,
since you want to bring all men
  in one hope to one table
  in your eternal kingdom.

THURSDAY AFTER THE EPIPHANY

TODAY
1 Jn 4:19–5:4: How does one become a child of God? First of all, by believing in Christ Jesus and then, if we claim to love God, we must also love our brothers, because we cannot claim to love God without loving his children. Giving our faith to Christ means also trusting those for whom Christ died when he revealed the love of God. Anyone who does not passionately love his brothers cannot claim to love God. That is a hard lesson for many people to learn, especially if they give priority to worshipping God and turn away from their fellow men.

But "anyone who has been begotten by God has already overcome the world." Surely this should make us burst forth into song—a hymn of victory. God's commandment is not a burden that we have to carry. We are in communion with one another, just as "we are in union with the Father and with his Son Jesus Christ" (1:3). Our joy, then, should be complete (see Jn 15:11; 16:24).

Ps 72: see the Tuesday after Epiphany.

Lk 4:14–22a: The scene is "a synagogue on the sabbath day," a place where Israel has again and again recognized its future in the words of the prophets. Now all eyes are fixed on Jesus as he "unrolls the scroll of the prophet Isaiah" and finds a passage that deeply concerns him. It is a message of tenderness and light—God is speaking once again to his people. Jesus is there: good news for the poor when the Lord lets himself be stripped of everything on the cross, and freedom for captives when he breaks open the entrance to the tomb.

So it was in "a synagogue on the sabbath day." But the horizon was already shining in the dawn when the Servant took all the misery of the world onto himself. Happy is the man who wakes up to those words—he will see the light of God.

■

When were we born? We do not mean: When did I utter that first inarticulate cry? but rather: What in my life was the word that decided my future? What was the word that committed me forever?

Was it when the Spirit seized hold of me and gave me the mission that called for the whole of my life? True life is, after all, only experienced in the perspective of a creative faithfulness. It is always an opening out of a moment when God put on my lips a word that was identified with myself, a word that was not a slogan, an argument or a speech, but action and life itself, a word that was always new.

Jesus was born in the Jordan, with his mission. There the Spirit of God came down on him and stayed with him, and from that moment on his mission merged into his life. The good news that he was to proclaim was gradually fulfilled in him. Christ did not impress himself on his listeners by means of his rhetoric or eloquence, nor did he have the authority of a scribe, but he fulfilled God's plan by taking it onto himself. He came, in other words, "to bring the good news to the poor," which means that he was the first to come poor and deprived of everything and to go as far as dying forsaken by everyone. He "proclaimed liberty to captives," which means that, in his resurrection, everyone who believes in him receives the spirit of liberty and rebirth.

It was enough for him to say one word to change a man's whole state, and the only response that he required was a word of sincere commitment. "Follow me," was all he said. "Follow me today. Wait no longer! The Word is fulfilled for you today. Today is the day when God and man meet each other."

How could the Church speak a different language after this? There is no need for subtle arguments, since the word entrusted to us is "something alive and active" (Heb 4:12). Each one of us can in fact say to his brothers: "This word is being fulfilled today," and it is being fulfilled for you. It is not an act of pride to say that, but an act of faith in the one who has called us. But unhappily the apostle so often loses faith in his own origins, moves further and further away from his birth, takes fright and is guilty of more and more postponements and delays. But it is labor lost. The only solution is to go back to the source. If we make room for the workings of the Spirit, we shall certainly be able to say: "This word is being fulfilled today," and that word will take us at once from our birth to the total gift and from our first word to that decisive word that will set the seal on our existence.

If we are to speak in the name of God, surely we must live each day as God's *today* and rediscover every moment of our lives a word that is always new—a word that is a new birth.

■

Your Word is being fulfilled today
  and your Spirit is renewing us.
Lord,
  may our lives proclaim peace and joy,
  light that is stronger than darkness,
  freedom received from your hands
  and you, our God,
  for ever and ever.

Let us live every day, Lord,
  as though it was the first and the last day.
May our lives be bathed
  in the source of our youth
  and may all our activities
  be full of the power of your resurrection.

FRIDAY AFTER THE EPIPHANY

WATER AND BLOOD
1 Jn 5:5–13: According to the heresy that divided the Church when this epistle was written, the Spirit entered Jesus' being at the time of his baptism. In the Jordan, the gnostics taught, the water flowed over the Son of God. But they also taught that the same Spirit left Jesus at the time of his passion. It was simply a man, not the Son of God, who gave his blood on the cross.

John refused to accept this teaching and insisted that Christ was one: "Any spirit which will not say this [that Jesus has come in the flesh] is not from God" (4:3). "The Spirit, the water and the blood . . . all three of them agree" and form one testimony. The Jesus who suffered on the cross is the same Jesus who was baptized. The water of the Jordan and the blood of the cross bathed the same body. The Spirit also does not speak on his own account, but communicates what he has received from the risen Lord and leads men to the "complete truth' (Jn 16:13). He manifests the unity that exists in Christ, true God and true man.

Ps 148: No other people have ever been blessed by the Lord like the Israelites. This hymnic psalm praises the special bond between God, his people and Jerusalem.

Lk 5:12–16: A leper—a man who was dead, but still alive. One day, before he had met Jesus, he became aware of a little spot shining on his side, a patch which grew until it covered his hands and his face, just as sin gnaws into the soul. Human society is always ready to erect barriers, and he was soon excluded.

Jesus came and took his place. He took human suffering onto himself to such a degree that men ultimately took him out of their city and thrust him into the world of the dead. Great crowds of people came from Galilee and Judea, Jerusalem and Idumea, the land beyond the Jordan and the country around Tyre and Sidon to see and hear him and to be healed—the sick, the crippled, the paralyzed—and they were all healed.

■

Water was always flowing for the many different ablutions given to satisfy a selfish need for purity. But confronted with a leper, a man whose very flesh was tainted, they had no solution and could only excommunicate him—banish him from their society. The Pharisees were not even moved to tenderness by the blood of the Son of Man when it was shed outside the walls of the holy city. They had countless ablutions, and all were quite useless. They did not comfort those who suffered, not from legal impurity, but from diseases of the flesh. What an empty religion that encouraged the soul but rejected the body!

But in Jordan the water had flowed over the Son of God like a new source, and he had immersed himself in it, taking on to himself the burden of his fellow men. Then, for the water of ritual purification, he had given the wine of the new convenant, anticipating the hour when his flesh and blood would be the sacrament of that covenant with all men. He threw himself wholeheartedly into humanity, healing lepers

without being afraid to touch them and purifying sinners without being frightened of loving them. Instead of religion, he gave pity and tenderness, the water of the Spirit and the blood of his cross. Sent away to join the dead, he opened the way of life for his brothers.

"Who can overcome the world?" Surely, only those who believe in him. The world with its cruelty, its selfishness and its rejected lepers thinks it can run away from death by ignoring death. But God has borne witness against that world, and his testimony is his blood, shed in love, water, the source of life in the desert of the world, and the Spirit, who raises the dead to life in the name of the Son of God. God has borne witness against this world and now he calls on us to bear witness too. May our faith in Christ be a commitment to the service of those who suffer. May our words become flesh and blood increasingly with the passage of time. May we too embrace the leper as our brother who is loved by God. And may our prayer be the place where we are strengthened in our belonging to that God who was made flesh for the salvation of the world.

■

God and Father of all men,
  you have given us your Son,
  the face of your love.
He has shared our human condition
  in all things
  and he has taken on himself
  the suffering of the rejected.
We ask you
  to give us a living faith in his incarnation,
  so that we too may be for our brothers
  the face and the word of your salvation.

SATURDAY AFTER THE EPIPHANY

PERFECT JOY

1 Jn 5:14–21: In the epilogue to his Letter, the apostle reviews the themes he has discussed and especially that of the inner law followed by the believer. What are the consequences of that law? First of all, the man who observes the commandments cannot ask for anything that is not "in accordance with God's will." Then he should be confident that his prayer will be answered when he prays for the antichrists who believe in the false gnostic teaching.

The true believer, the man who believes in Christ Jesus and who loves his brother, belongs to God. He can know God, and knowing God is entering into a personal relationship and living in communion with him. He should be on his guard against idols and the teaching of those antichrists, who have replaced God with a lie and whose satanic doctrine leads to eternal death.

Ps 150 invites believers to dance and be happy, because God will lead them to victory.

Jn 3:22–30: John baptized at Aenon, "where there was plenty of water," while Jesus was baptizing in Judea. Seeing both of them baptizing, a man thought: They are competing with each other! But his heart was hardened. He did not see with the eyes of his heart. Had he done so, he would have seen that the water that Jesus was using was water "welling up to eternal life" (4:14). But John saw with the eyes of his heart. It is clear from his words that he had recognized the One sent by God. And so he was glad to retire into the background and to make way for the Bridegroom.

∎

"A man can only lay claim to what is given him from heaven." What wonderful words of faith spoken by the Baptist! There is only one sin that can lead us to death and that is to attribute everything to ourselves and ask God for nothing. Because of this statement and one other, he is perhaps the greatest of all saints. The other statement is a definition of his own holiness: "I am the Bridegroom's

friend." His is a holiness that is full of joy and love, a holiness that puts him in his rightful place, a place that is both humble and great.

"The Bridegroom's friend!" Everything in the new covenant is proclaimed in terms of love and wedding, communion and life. Jesus is the Bridegroom. He loves us to the point of handing his body over to us so that we may be one in him. All love bears his sign and all love is directed toward him. In that astonishing covenant, everything is transfigured and every being is loved by God, in Jesus the beloved Son. No one can ever again lay claim to anything as his own—everything comes to us "from heaven." We receive everything from God. Married couples receive each other from each other, but only in the name of the living God who makes their love holy. Parents and children, masters and servants, young people and adults, pastors and lay people—they are all given to each other by the love of God who makes all things new. A festive air hovers over the world, and as each one of us grows smaller for the other to grow greater, so each one grows while God looks at us. We are all, like the Baptist, forerunners of the good news for each other, and we perform that task in the translucent joy of friendship.

One baptizes here while the other baptizes there. What does it matter? One person lives his faith in one way and another expresses it differently. Everything is grace—at least as long as each one of us lives as a friend of the Bridegroom. Do two friends have to be so like each other that they are indistinguishable—or that they compete with each other for the higher position? The holiness of certain people throws light on that of others who are holy in a different and yet in the same way, like the various sounds in a symphony that together form a great work. Play, you lutes and harps and cymbals! You are all necessary for the feast. A new world is born—can you not hear the voice of the Bridegroom? Happy is the man who stays awake for the wedding feast. He will know true joy. There is, after all, only one sin that leads to death, and that is to shut oneself off in sadness, as though God had never renewed everything in Jesus Christ.

∎

Do not let us, Lord,
　make an exclusive claim to your Son,
　as though he belonged to us alone.

Make our hearts so joyful
   that we want to give him to our brothers,
   so that they too will know the peace
   that you give to those you invite
   to the feast of your covenant,
   in humility and truth—
   in Jesus Christ our Lord.

CELEBRATING THE SAINTS' DAYS
THROUGHOUT THE YEAR

Holy Father,
you are glorified in the assembly of the saints:
when you crown their merits,
you crown your own gifts (Preface of the Saints I).

The tone of the lectionary for the feasts and commemorations of the saints is very discreet—the only obligatory readings are those for the feasts and certain commemorations of saints mentioned in the New Testament. On other saints' days, we are advised not to neglect the continuous reading of the ferial lectionary unless we have a special reason. We have decided to respect this option, and references to biblical readings will be found in this section only in certain cases. We have also not provided any exegetical comments, since it is in most cases possible to refer to one of the many books devoted to the weekday lectionary for these.

It is difficult to resist the temptation to draw portraits throughout the year of the saints commemorated by the Church, including those who do not have a place of honor in the universal calendar but are nonetheless universally known and venerated. At the same time, however, it is important not to repeat what has been said very well by others in their introduction to missals or books of the hours and in detailed studies. The reader can consult many books of this kind if he so wishes. We have therefore chosen a middle way, which is suggestive rather than complete, and have simply tried to place these saints in their context or the world in which they lived and to quote here and there from their works.

JANUARY

2 *Basil the Great and Gregory of Nazianzus.* These two monks were both born in families of saints, and they became friends after studying together in Athens. They played an important part in the life of the Church in the fourth century, at a time when it had freedom, but was divided by dogmatic differences about the divinity of Christ. Basil, who became the bishop of Caesarea in Cappadocia, was before this a master of the monastic life. In his rule monasticism was based on well structured little communities living in poverty. He also wrote very decisively in defense of the poor and a magnificent treatise on the Holy Spirit. Gregory was the patriarch of Constantinople, but he chose to withdraw to Nazianzus to escape from the intrigues of his adversaries, who could not endure his vehement defense of dogma. His homilies on the Trinity have great mystical depth.

> To the hungry belongs the bread that you hold in reserve; to the barefoot, the shoes that are rotting in your home; to the needy, the money that you keep buried (Basil).

> The Spirit is my intimate friend and I spend my present life inviting others, as far as I can, to worship the Father, the Son and the Holy Spirit (Gregory).

3 *Geneviève of Paris.* Nanterre was no more than a village when Geneviève was born there about 420. She consecrated herself when she was very young to God and lived in Paris, which was at that time only an island in the Seine. The hearts of the people of Paris were won over by her self-abandonment and her strength and by her reputation for holiness, and she saved them by her prayer from Attila's hordes when they turned their attention to Gaul. The abbey that was built in her name on Mount Saint Geneviève was unfortunately destroyed between 1802 and 1807, and before then, in November 1793, the revolutionaries had thrown her ashes into the Seine.

13 *Hilary of Poitiers,* who lived in the fourth century, was the spiritual father of St. Martin, the bishop of Poitiers and the author of the first important work of theology in the West, *De Trinitate*. Like so many other defenders of the faith, he experienced exile and poverty.

> Give me, almighty God, a true understanding of words, the light of intelligence and faith in truth, so that I am able to tell men what I believe.

15 *Remigius* was bishop of Rheims in the sixth century. He baptized Clovis I and his people, thus making France Christian. He played an important part in evangelizing the people and in setting up the Church in northern Gaul. The abbey that was built in his name at Rheims became famous.

17 *Antony of Egypt*. In the fourth century, when the bishop of Alexandria, Athanasius, was struggling to defend the divinity of Christ, Antony heard the words of the Gospel: "If you wish to be perfect, go and sell what you own and give the money to the poor . . . then come, follow me" (Mt 19:21). He retired to the desert and lived ascetically, praying constantly. With all the desert fathers, his disciples, he reminds us that our real struggle is against hidden forces that, by attacking God, destroy man. In the desert, he proclaimed the essential good news.

> There are men who seem to remain silent, but who speak all the time because their hearts condemn others. And there are men who, speaking from morning till night, always remain silent because they do not say a single word that edifies those who hear them (*Apophthegmata Patrum*).

21 *Agnes*. Should this Roman girl, who was martyred under Diocletian (305 A.D.), be called "pure" (*agnos* in Greek) or "lamb" (*agnus* in Latin)? Nowadays in Rome, where her memory is kept alive, the Pope blesses two spotless lambs, whose wool is used to decorate the vestments of archbishops (the pallium).

22 *Vincent*. The cult of this martyr of Saragossa, who died in the fourth century, has been kept alive in Spain. His name means "victor."

24 *Francis de Sales*. Born in Savoy, this nobleman gave up a career in the law and, steeped in the Franciscan tradition, entered the Church and became bishop of Geneva in 1593. He was one of the leaders of the

Catholic Counter-Reformation, and his first mission took him to the Calvinists, whose almost inhuman severity disturbed him. He always remained opposed to the strict doctrine of predestination and preached instead the Catholic "dogma" of trust between God and man, in this way speaking a language that was understood by lay people in search of the spiritual life. His *Introduction to the Devout Life* was and still is a monument of Christian spirituality and humanism. He is the patron saint of writers and journalists.

25 *The Conversion of the Apostle Paul.*

Readings: Acts 22:3–16 or 9:1–22
          Ps 117
          Mk 16:15–18

He was wrapped in a great light which blinded him until he regained his sight in the water of baptism. He believed that he was clear-sighted and honest, and that he defended God's cause jealously and passionately. He was so opposed to heresy and false teaching that he had those who followed Jesus Christ punished. Acting on information he had received that the Christian sect had firm roots in Damascus, he hurried to the town, but after his experience on the road he had to be led there. He spent three days in darkness, thinking about the call he had received, and on the third day he regained his sight and at once began preaching to the Jews that Jesus was the Messiah. The risen Christ had raised up the apostle so that he could extend the frontiers of the Church to include every part of the known world and the people who walked in darkness might receive the great light and hope that comes from faith (see Is 9:1).

26 *Timothy and Titus*, Paul's disciples.

First reading: 2 Tim 1:1–8 or Tit 1:1–5

Succession in the Church was given form with Timothy and Titus. Unity is not automatic in the Church. There must be overseers with oversight over that unity. They are the "bishops" to whom God gives a spirit of power, love and reason to enable them to govern his house. From century to century, the laying on of hands in the Church points to the gift of the Spirit with the Church's unity in faith in mind. Ordination does do away with the great freedom of charisms which every baptized Christian has from the Spirit, but it makes it possible for those charisms to bear fruit in the unity of the one body of Christ.

27 *Angela Merici.* During the Renaissance, the Christian humanist was led by her concern for the education of poor girls to found a teaching order, the Ursulines, whose religious life would be very flexible, not enclosed and without any useless rules. Her original idea was soon made to conform, however, to more traditional norms.

> God has given free will to everyone and he wishes to do violence to no one, but he only suggests, invites and advises.

28 *Thomas Aquinas.* The man the Western Church regards as its leading thinker was large, calm, brilliantly intelligent and deeply mystical. He was a member of a noble family and became a Benedictine oblate at Monte Cassino before displeasing his family by joining the Order of Preachers, recently founded by Saint Dominic. He studied at Cologne, Paris and Rome and became a master of theology in Paris, despite the many traps set for him by rival secular masters and his own keen ear for new questions confronting theology in the recent rediscovery of Aristotle's philosophy coupled with his rigorous application of reason in the elaboration of faith. His aim was always to harmonize faith and reason, piety and doctrine, without confusing them. He died in 1274. His work was held in suspicion for a long time, but eventually became the basis for the official theology of the Church.

31 *John Bosco.* Young people presented the Church with a serious problem as early as the beginning of the nineteenth century, when Don Bosco founded the Salesian Order with the aim of providing adolescents with an education adapted to their social condition. He was especially concerned with poor and less gifted children. The part played by John Bosco and his Salesians in the development of contemporary education cannot be overemphasized, nor is it possible to overestimate the importance for the Church to be at one with young people at a time like the present, when economic crises and the resulting unemployment inevitably first affect those who are the most poor.

FEBRUARY

2 *The Presentation of Jesus in the Temple.*

Readings: Mal 3:1–4 or Heb 2:14–18
Ps 24:7–10
Lk 2:22–40

See the commentaries on December 29 and 30.

3 *Blase.* This saint is believed to have cured a child who was choking over a fish bone. For this reason he is often invoked for disorders of the throat. What is perhaps more important is that this almost unknown fourth-century martyr was Armenian. He belonged therefore to an almost forgotten people who have for a very long time been victims of a terrible genocide.

3 *Anskar.* In the fourth century, Anskar (or Oscar), a monk of Corbie in Picardy, went to Corbie in Saxony as a monk and afterward became the bishop of Hamburg and the papal legate among the Nordic people, devoting his energies there to the spread of the Gospel. He has been described as an apostle externally and a monk within, thus fulfilling a fine evangelical ideal.

5 *Agatha.* Legend surrounds this well-known Sicilian saint, whose name means "good." She was martyred during the reign of Emperor Decius at the end of the third century A.D.

6 *Paul Miki and His Companions.* All twenty-five of them were crucified at Nagasaki in Japan in 1597. Less than half a century had passed since the great mission of Francis Xavier, but Christians were already dying for Christ. Three of those crucified were Japanese Jesuits, six were Spanish Franciscan and the rest were Japanese lay people, three of them children.

10 *Scholastica.* She was St. Benedict's sister and shares with him the honor of initiating cenobitic monasticism in the West. She was born at Norcia in Umbria and joined her brother at Monte Cassino, meeting him frequently there for edifying conversations. She died there in 543 A.D.

11 *Our Lady of Lourdes.* The message of Lourdes echoes the Gospel: "Be converted and pray without ceasing!" Since the time of the apparitions there in the middle of the nineteenth century, Lourdes has been an important center of prayer, return to the Gospel and comfort for the poor and the sick.

14 *Cyril and Methodius* are the patrons, with St. Benedict, of Europe. These two missionaries, who were brothers, had an extraordinarily adventurous life in central Europe. They were the sons of a senior public servant in Thessalonica and, after living as monks in Bythinia, were sent on various missions in Moravia, with the aim of establishing the Church there. They invented an alphabet that could be used for translating the Bible and celebrating the liturgy—the Glagolitic or Cyrillic alphabet. It helped them to celebrate in the language of the people. They encountered opposition from the Germanic missionaries, who regarded them as competitors and preferred to celebrate in Latin, in order to give honor to the court of the emperor. Rome supported them and strengthened their authority, but Methodius was still imprisoned for three years. In the meantime, Cyril died in Rome in 869. Methodius died in Slavic territory in 885. They succeeded in establishing the use of the Slavonic language of the people in the liturgy without at the same time, as the first reading for their feast tells us, falsifying the word of God.

18 *Bernadette Soubirous.* This girl from a poor family, the eldest of six children, was in charge of the flocks and well balanced and intelligent, although uneducated. The Immaculate Virgin revealed herself to her at Lourdes in 1858, and nothing could ever make Bernadette doubt what she had seen and heard. She spent her life away from the crowds, in the house of the Sisters of Charity at Nevers in France, where she performed very humble tasks, according to the will of her superior. She died, invoking Mary, in 1879.

22 *The Chair of Saint Peter.*

Readings: 1 Pet 5:1–4
           Ps 23
           Mt 16:13–19

Peter did not have the chair of a scribe or a doctor of the law. His was the chair of a humble shepherd who gave his life, like Jesus himself, for his sheep. He undoubtedly knew poverty before he was martyred. That is how the Church was built up. The foundation stone was laid on

Calvary and its living stones are formed of the faith of those who believe in Christ. It was therefore only right that the apostle Peter should have been the first to share in the cross of Christ. In so doing, he strengthened his brothers' faith.

23 *Polycarp.* The martyrdom of the bishop of Smyrna in 155 A.D. is narrated in a well authenticated account. It forms a link between the second century Church and the apostles, since, if Polycarp did not know the apostle John, he certainly knew those who were close to him. He was eighty-six when he died.

> Lord, Father of your beloved child, Jesus Christ, I bless you for having regarded me as being worthy of this day and this hour, as worthy to be one of your martyrs and to share in the cup of your Christ. May I be admitted to your presence as a pleasing sacrifice, prepared and manifested by you in advance and brought about by you, who are the true God without falsehood. (These words are reputed to have been spoken by Polycarp at the moment of death.)

MARCH

4 *Casimir.* This prince, who lived between 1458 and 1484, dying very young of consumption, is the patron saint of Poland and Lithuania. He was born in Cracow. He defended the poor and loved and venerated the Virgin Mary.

17 *Patrick.* The patron saint of Ireland was certainly a very great man. He was born toward the end of the fourth century and fled to Gaul. One of the places he visited was Auxerre, where he was consecrated bishop. He left there to go back to Ireland to evangelize the country. Despite resistance to his message and great hostility, he became very popular during his lifetime and has remained so ever since. It was from Ireland that missionaries, monks living a very austere life, came to the continent in the sixth century to strengthen the Church there. They continued to found centers of religious life throughout the whole of the Middle Ages.

19 *Joseph,* Spouse of the Virgin Mary.

Readings: 2 Sam 7:4–5a, 12–14a, 16
Ps 89

Rom 4:14, 16–18, 22
Mt 1:16, 18–21, 24a or Lk 2:41–51a

See the commentary on December 18.

25 *The Annunciation of the Lord.*

Readings: Is 7:10–14
Ps 40
Heb 10:4–10
Lk 1:26–38

See the commentary on December 20.

APRIL

4 *Isidore of Seville.* This was a great intellectual, whose works were read and studied everywhere in Europe throughout the High Middle Ages, to such an extent that his period was known as the "Isidorian rebirth." As the bishop of Seville, he had oversight of the Visigothic Church at the peak of its prosperity in the seventh century. He laid the foundations for the local Mozarabic liturgy, and above all he wrote such great works as the *Origin of Certain Things,* a veritable encyclopedia of knowledge, *In Praise of Spain,* and the *Sententiae,* which were used as a manual at theological colleges. His relics are preserved at León, where an abbey was built and is regarded as a national sanctuary in Spain.

7 *John Baptist de la Salle.* This very well educated canon from Rheims (1651–1719) had been trained by the Sulpicians and had entered the world of education himself, but he became aware of the ignorance of the children of the poor who were not able to study. Gathering a number of companions around him, he founded the Congregation of the Brothers of the Christian Schools with the aim of providing an education for the poorest children. His schools have played an important part in the history of education, but the founder had to withdraw when defamation occurred.

16 *Benedict Joseph Labre.* This eighteenth century saint lived a strange, wandering life of abject poverty, despised by everyone, in an age dominated by philosophy and reason. He was born in Artois and

wanted to be a monk, but was rejected by most communities and therefore spent his life as a mendicant pilgrim, traveling throughout Europe. Italy was the only country to welcome him, and he often stayed at Loretto and in Rome. He ended his life in the ruins of the Colosseum and died in the back room of a butcher's shop at the age of thirty-five.

21 *Anselm.* One of the great intellectuals of the Middle Ages, Anselm was born at Aosta in 1033. He lived for a long time in Normandy in the abbey at Bec, where he studied and later became abbot. The abbey had close connections with England and he was appointed primate of Canterbury. As archbishop, he set about the task of reforming the Church in England in accordance with the canons of the Gregorian Reform, but when he encountered hostility from William II and Henry I, he had to go into exile. His theology occupies a place halfway between the speculative thought of the Church Fathers and the rational, dialectic thinking of the Scholastics and can be summed up in the famous words *Fides quaerens intellectum*—"Faith in search of understanding." His thought ranges from the theme of proof of the existence of God and the idea of God to that of the mystery of the incarnation, as depicted in his *Cur Deus homo?* ("Why did God become man?")

23 *George.* Very little that can be accepted as fully authentic is known about this great Eastern martyr, who died about 303 A.D. and is the patron saint of Greece, England, knights and armies. What is known is that he fascinated the crusaders and that many legends surround his life, the most famous being his triumph over the dragon.

25 *Mark.* He is the patron saint of Venice. He died, it would seem, in Alexandria, from where his relics were apparently brought. He died a martyr's death. His name is above all associated with the second Gospel, in which the question that is fundamental to our faith is asked again and again: "Who is the man Jesus?"

Readings: 1 Pet 5:5b–14
Ps 89
Mk 16:15–20

29 *Catherine of Siena.* Catherine Benincasa's life was in no sense ordinary. She was very well known in Siena, where she was visited by

many people. A Dominican tertiary who lived in poverty, she was a very cheerful woman but also very holy. But there was great suffering outside Siena. The Pope and the cardinals had been in Avignon for so long. The Italian cities were hostile to each other. Catherine went to Avignon. She had great skill as a preacher and had the gift of ecstatic prayer. Gregory XI was overcome by her persuasion and returned to Rome, but the French were displeased and raised up an antipope, Clement VII, soon after the election of Urban VI, Gregory's successor. This was the beginning of the "Great Schism." Catherine went again to Rome, but died there after a painful illness. She was thirty-three at her death in 1380.

> Holy and gentle father in Christ, the gentle Jesus, I am writing to you. . . . Be patient when you are told these things, because they are only said for God's honor and your salvation. . . . Your authority extends to everyone, but your vision is limited and human. . . . I know Your Holiness longs to have helpers who can serve you, but you must listen to them patiently (Letter to Urban VI).

MAY

2 *Athanasius.* Patriarch of Alexandria in the fourth century, Athanasius was exiled five times for having defended unwaveringly the divinity of Jesus in opposition to the Arians. (See January 1.) Perhaps his most striking statement is this: "God became man so that man might become the son of God." If Christ were not really God, how, Athanasius asked, could we be made through him participants in the true life of God? He also encouraged the growth of monasticism and wrote a life of Antony of Egypt. (See January 17.)

3 *Philip and James,* Apostles.

Readings: 1 Cor 15:1–8
Ps 19a
Jn 14:6–14

"The next day, after Jesus had decided to leave for Galilee, he met Philip and said, 'Follow me.' Philip came from the same town, Bethsaida, as Andrew and Peter" (Jn 1:43–44). "Philip found

Nathanael and said to him, 'We have found the one Moses wrote about in the law, the one about whom the prophets wrote: he is Jesus, son of Joseph, from Nazareth.' 'From Nazareth?' said Nathanael. 'Can anything good come from that place?' 'Come and see,' replied Philip" (Jn 1:45–46). "Among those who went up to worship at the festival were some Greeks. These approached Philip, who came from Bethsaida in Galilee, and put this question to him, 'Sir, we should like to see Jesus.' Philip went to tell Andrew, and Andrew and Philip went together to tell Jesus" (Jn 12:20–21) . "Philip said, 'Lord, let us see the Father and we shall be satisfied.' 'Have I been with you all this time, Philip,' said Jesus to him, 'and you still do not know me? To have seen me is to have seen the Father' " (Jn 14:8–9).

Nothing certain is known about James, the son of Alpheus. It is also not certain whether he should be identified with James, the "Lord's brother," to whom a New Testament epistle is attributed and who led the Church in Jerusalem.

14 *Matthias,* Apostle. He was elected after the Lord's ascension to replace Judas and to complete the number twelve. From this choice (see the first reading), it is clear that Matthias must have been a "witness to the resurrection" of Jesus and also a companion of Jesus during his life on earth when he was preaching. It is also important to notice how it is left to the Spirit to point to the man who was to join the apostles in their ministry. The symbolic value of the number twelve, which takes the Church back to the people of God in the Old Testament, is also stressed in this reading.

19 *Ivo.* A canon lawyer from Brittany, he is, naturally enough, the patron saint of lawyers. He was born in 1253, became a priest, and his pastoral care of the poor consisted in his acting as a judge in the ecclesiastical courts and in running a hospice on the family manor at Kermartin.

22 *Rita.* She is the patron saint of desperate causes and her cult is extremely popular. She can even be asked for the grace of patience. Born at Cascia in Umbria in 1381, she made a vow of virginity at the age of twelve but obeyed her parents and married. She endured her husband's brutality for eighteen years, until he was murdered. She lost her two sons and finally became an Augustinian nun in Cascia. She

was stigmatized on the forehead, and the wound was so putrid that she had to live in isolation, seeing only the sick whom she healed.

25 *The Venerable Bede.* Newman called this eighth century English saint the model of the Benedictine life. The first Anglo-Saxon scholar, his influence was felt throughout the West. He wrote works both of theology and of history.

25 *Gregory VII.* The name of this great Pope (1028–1085) is always linked with the so-called Gregorian Reform, which aimed to bring the Church, which had followed the wrong direction because of the system of lay investitures conferred by the emperor and princes on bishops and abbots, back to the right path. Gregory, who had been a monk and abbot of the Roman church of St. Paul Outside-the-Walls and then a counselor of the reforming Popes, was unusually committed to the task of purifying the Church, even to the point of opposing Emperor Henry IV, who, despite his repentance at Canossa, still wanted to control the Church. Gregory died in exile at Salerno.

26 *Philip Neri.* This saint was humorous as well as tender. But humor is a form of tenderness, and he often made people laugh in order to escape from manifestations of the Spirit that disturbed him and others too much—he experienced unexpected states of ecstasy from time to time. Yet he was the most human of saints and very active. As a priest in Rome, he gathered a community of fellow priests around himself. These became the "Oratory," which was a place of unprecedented pastoral inventiveness. It was there, for example, that the musical form known as the "Oratorio" was invented, consisting originally of music improvised by the people present listening to the preacher and often borrowing tunes that were already well known and applying them to the texts in the preacher's sermon. Philip Neri was actively involved in the Catholic Counter-Reformation. When he died in 1595, he had played a very important part in restoring not only an exacting, but also a very optimistic faith.

27 *Augustine of Canterbury.* The meeting between Pope John Paul II and the archbishop of Canterbury at Whitsun in 1982 was a memorable occasion. They claimed to be the successors of Gregory the Great and St. Augustine. The latter was a monk of St. Andrew at the Coelius in Rome. He ws sent with his companions to England by Pope Gregory

with the task of planting the seed of faith there. There was a good harvest. The Pope had advised the missionaries to respect the local customs and to try to breathe the spirit of the Gospel into them. Augustine became the first archbishop of Canterbury. He died there in or about 605 A.D.

30 *Joan of Arc.* This peasant girl from Lorraine was already a firm believer when, at the age of thirteen, she "heard" Michael the Archangel and then St. Catherine and St. Margaret speak of the sad state of France and urge her to arouse the "little king of Burgundy," Charles VII. Orléans had almost fallen into the hands of the English. Joan eventually met the king and obtained a military uniform from him. She raised an army for the king and led it to several victories. Then she took Charles VII to Rheims and had him consecrated king, according to the French tradition. But her Calvary was soon to commence: she was taken prisoner by the people of Burgundy, sold to the English, judged at Rouen and condemned as a witch, a heretic and a schismatic. Bishop Cauchon refused to recognize her faithfulness and intelligence, and she was finally handed over to the secular arm and burned alive on May 30, 1431. Her ashes were thrown into the Seine.

I rely on God for everything. I would be the most unhappy woman in the world if I did not know I was in God's grace.

31 *The Visitation of the Virgin Mary.*

Readings: Zeph 3:14–18a or Rom 12:9–16b
Is 12:4–6
Lk 1:39–56

See the commentaries on December 21 and 22.

JUNE
1 *Justin.* The tolerant but philosophically inclined Antonines ruled in Rome in the second century A.D. Justin, a rhetor, found the pagan philosophy disappointing and turned to the Christian faith, putting all his intellectual gifts at its service. He tried to unite the tradition of the

Greek philosophers with the Christian faith. He worked out an approach to a theology of the Word, the Logos. As an optimist, he recognized that man's first introduction to eternal truth was through his reason, even though he had to come to the light of the Word made flesh before he could gain access to that truth. Justin died a martyr's death, saying: "No one, if he is intelligent, abandons the truth for error." He affirmed the truth in public when he was dying and during his life by writing open letters or "apologies" to the emperor. These are still an important source of knowledge about the early Church.

2 *Pothinus, Blandina and Their Companions.* The people of Lyons expressed their hatred of Christians living in the Rhone valley in 177 A.D., during the reign of Emperor Marcus Aurelius. During the pagan feasts in the city, they put to death Pothinus, the ninety year old bishop, and the young slave girl who was comforting him, Blandina. Their martyrdom is known to us from a letter written by the Christians of Lyons and Vienne to the churches of Asia and Phrygia, from which most of them had originally come.

> We were all afraid for Blandina, because she was so weak. But she was filled with such power that she ended by exhausting her executioners. It was sufficient for her simply to say again and again: "I am a Christian and there is no evil among us," and she regained strength.

3 *Charles Lwanga and His Companions.* The first African martyrs were burned alive like living torches by a depraved local ruler in Uganda toward the end of the nineteenth century. There were twenty-two of them, some Roman Catholics, others Anglicans.

5 *Boniface.* Wynfrith, an English monk, landed on the Frisian coast in the eighth century. His task was to evangelize the continent of Europe. He was given the name of Boniface by Pope Gregory II, who also confirmed his mission. As the apostle of Frisia and Germany, he established bases for the Church with the help of several monks who had also come from England. He became archbishop of Mainz about 747. He also worked, with less success, to reorganize the Frankish Church, in accordance with the wish of Pepin the Short, whom he anointed in 751, thus endorsing, with the approval of Rome, the coup d'état of the first Carolingian against the Merovingian kings. He then

returned to his mission among the Frisians. He was martyred in Frisia in 755, at the age of eighty. His body rests in the abbey at Fulda, which he wanted to be the center from which Christianity radiated throughout Germany.

6 *Norbert.* This noble Rhinelander, a convert to the Gospel of Christ, is one of the many reformers of religious life in the Middle Ages. He gathered together a number of disciples in the valley of Prémontré—in the "desert"—near Laon. These men soon became priests and lived together in communities as "canons regular." Later, Norbert became archbishop of Magdeburg. He died in 1134.

9 *Ephrem.* The man who was known as the "cithara of the Holy Spirit" was a deacon at Edessa in Persia in the fourth century. He wrote many works, both theological and lyrical, testifying to the vivacity of faith at that time beyond the frontiers of the Roman Empire.

11 *Barnabas.* We have to do justice to this "son of encouragement" (that is what his name means), without whom Paul might never have become the great missionary that he was. This Jerusalem Christian was a man with an open mind who quickly grasped that it was enough for pagans to believe in order to accept them into the Church. He was made responsible for the mission at Antioch, and it was to that town that he took the convert, Saul of Tarsus. It was from Antioch too that Paul's first mission set off. The story of this "sending off" on missionary work in Acts (see the reading for today) is very meaningful, since it links that mission with the inspiration of the Holy Spirit and the Church's responsibility, made tangible in the laying on of hands.

Reading: Acts 11:21b–26; 13:1–3.

13 *Anthony of Padua.* Devotions to saints are in order so long as they do not distort the true image too much. Has that happened in the case of Anthony of Padua? This noble Portuguese was in a sense the favorite son of Francis of Assisi, who was afraid that his order might be changed by intellectuals and who entrusted Anthony with the task of teaching theology to the priests in the order because he was not only learned, but also a saint and truly poor. But Anthony was also a missionary and an outstanding preacher, visiting Morocco, the south of France, where there were many Albigenses, Italy and especially Padua, where he died in 1231. He was canonized after his death by Gregory IX.

21 *Aloysius Gonzaga.* A member of a noble Italian family, Aloysius became a Jesuit at the age of sixteen, but died when he was only twenty-three in 1591, a victim of his devotion to those stricken by the plague in Rome. He was characterized by extreme purity and a very simple form of holiness.

22 *John Fisher and Thomas More.* Both were victims of the king of England, Henry VIII, both were humanists and friends and both were martyred for their faithfulness to the Church. Fisher was the chancellor of Cambridge University and Erasmus' friend when he wrote his first refutation of Lutheranism. At that time he was supported by Henry VIII, but the tide soon turned when the king scorned the freedoms of the Church and wanted to divorce his wife. Rome was opposed to this and Henry demanded that he should be recognized as the head of the Anglican Church. Not only John Fisher, who had been created cardinal, but also Thomas More, the chancellor of England and a man with a very high reputation, resisted the king. Both were executed as traitors in 1535. More's *Utopia* is a masterpiece, describing an ideal form of government. Both men are venerated now as martyrs who were deeply attached to the Church and did not for that reason try to hide from themselves the problem of the distinctive nature of the Anglican approach to faith.

24 *The Birth of John the Baptist.* "A man came, sent by God. . . ." (Jn 1:6). Six months before the birth of Christ, the Church celebrates the birth of the forerunner, just at the time when the days begin to shorten. Was it not John who said of Jesus: "He must grow greater and I must grow smaller"? At every period of Christian history, the midsummer feast of John the Baptist has always been a time of great festivities, preceded by a day of fasting, at the end of which the first Eucharist, the Mass of the vigil, is celebrated.

Readings: Vigil: Jer 1:4–10
Ps 71
1 Pet 1:8–12
Lk 1:5–17

Day: Is 48:1–6
Ps 139
Acts 13:22–26
Lk 1:57–66, 80

See the commentaries on December 19, 23 and 24.

■

"Lord, you examine me and know me . . . you read my thoughts from far away" (Ps 139). John the Baptist is deeply conscious of God's presence. God is coming! God is there! He has to hurry to the meeting place and prepare the way of the Lord's coming in the desert. God is coming to judge mankind. "The axe is laid to the roots of the trees, the wheat is gathered . . . and the chaff will be burned in the fire" (Mt 3:10–12; cf. Lk 3:9). John is rough. When he was still very young he went to live in the desert as an ascetic. But we should look further at the psalm chosen for his feast: "I thank you for the wonder of myself, for the wonder of your works" (verse 14). If God examines man's thoughts, it is not primarily because he wants to judge him. Or rather, if he judges, he does so with the fire of love, to purify him and reveal the wonder of man as a creature of the living God and a child of the Father.

But who would dare to say with total self-assurance that he is entirely a "wonder" for God? John's name means "God is gracious." The "wonder" of man is above all that God does not judge him according to his human actions, but according to the unlimited extent of his own grace. Perhaps the Baptist had not grasped the full extent of that grace?

We can only answer this question by rereading the canticle that was sung, according to the evangelist, by John's father Zechariah: "God shows mercy to our ancestors and remembers his holy covenant. . . . Little child, you will go before the Lord to prepare the way for him, to give his people knowledge of salvation; this by the tender mercy of our God, who will bring the rising Sun to visit us" (Lk 2:72, 76–78).

27 *Cyril of Alexandria.* Cyril, a hermit, followed his uncle as patriarch of Alexandria in 412. He was in many ways a despotic man, but that was fully in accordance with the tradition of the Egyptian Church, which was confronted with the totalitarian claims made by Constantinople. Cyril in fact spent much of his life in vehement debate with Nestorius about the status of Mary as the "Mother of God" (see January 1). This conflict ended at the Council of Ephesus, but despite the ratification of the dogma by Rome, the Eastern Church remained divided for a long time between the "Cyrillians" and the "anti-Cyrillians."

28 *Irenaeus of Lyons.* Irenaeus was a disciple of Polycarp in Asia Minor who succeeded Pothinus as the bishop of Lyons (see June 2). His writings are extremely important, and it is because of them that he was known as "Irenaeus" (the "peaceful one"). The second century Church was divided by gnosticism—in other words, by attempts made by certain philosophers to minimize the incarnation of the Word in order to eliminate the mystery of a God who was made flesh. These men discredited history, life itself, the Old Testament and the structures of the Christian Church in attempting to retain no more than a spiritual aspect of faith, which was in any case wrong. Irenaeus reacted strongly against their theories and his treatise *Adversus haereses* is a monument to classical Catholic teaching, founded on firm faith, the apostolic tradition and the whole of Scripture. The feast of St. Irenaeus precedes that of Peter and Paul, and the eve of their feast is a good occasion to reflect about these words of Irenaeus:

> Although it is spread throughout the universe, the Church has received from the apostles and their disciples faith in one God and in one Jesus Christ, the Son of God, who became flesh, and in one Holy Spirit. That is the preaching that the Church has received and it preserves it carefully, as though it were living in one house. The languages of the world are certainly very different, but the strength of tradition is one and the same. Where the Church is, there is also the Spirit of God, and where the Spirit of God is, there is also the Church and all grace, for the Spirit is truth.

But the same saint also wrote these words:

> The glory of God is man alive, and man's life is to see God.

29 *Peter and Paul.* Both men died as martyrs, bearing witness to the Christian faith in Rome between 64 and 67 A.D. One was buried on the Vatican hill and the other outside the city on the road to Ostia. Throughout the centuries, there has been an unending pilgrimage to the sources of the Church in Rome. This pilgrimage to the tomb of the apostles is the act at the center of the bishops' pastoral visit to Rome, where they go to meet the Pope, the guardian of the apostolic tradition, according to the oldest formulation of the primacy of Rome.

Readings: Vigil: Acts 3:1–10
Ps 19a
Gal 1:11–20
Jn 21:15–19

Feast: Acts 12:1–11
Ps 34
2 Tim 4:6–8, 17–18
Mt 16:13–19

These two men, both pillars of the Church, seem to have been different in every way. Peter was a fisherman with rough hands, whereas Paul was a learned rabbi. Peter's attachment to Christ increased day by day as their association deepened. Paul was abruptly and dogmatically converted to the Lord. Their approach to faith was different—Peter's was patient and even hesitant in the case of admitting pagans to membership in the Church, while Paul preferred an audacious and even violent approach as the apostle of the Gentiles. On several occasions they were involved in sharp and almost acrimonious debate, and for a long time their paths hardly ever touched, Peter remaining in Jerusalem and Paul crossing the Mediterranean and Asia Minor. They came together in Rome—in death and in witnessing as martyrs to faith. It is in these two very different men that the Church recognizes the extent to which it has to be pulled one way and then the other by what is new and what is old, by caution and urgency and by the homeland and the mission field until that unity which is always just beyond the reach of human models is achieved.

"The good news preached is not a human message," Paul insists, but the Spirit is only able to speak through men living at a particular moment in time. The Gospel is a revelation by God, but those who proclaim it always have to be on their guard against the temptation to go further or interpret it individually. Jesus told Peter: "I will give you the keys of the kingdom of heaven," and the gatekeeper has, after all, to do everything possible to keep the gates open for everyone who is looking for life. "Whatever you loose on earth, Peter, shall be considered loosed in heaven." Faith is given to us to make us free. Is that a contradiction? No, it is not. But the Church simply continues throughout history to further this adventure, which is impossible for men but not for God: an adventure in which apparently irreconcilable opposites are brought together—the eternal and the everyday, the Spirit and our world, flesh and heaven, life and death—an adventure which the Church could never bring to a good end if it were not founded on Peter and Paul, on our earth which has been ploughed and sown so many times and on the invincible appeal of new horizons.

JULY

3 *Thomas.* According to tradition, Thomas went as far as Persia and India, where he preached to the Malabars. Even now, the Indians speak of the "Christians of Saint Thomas." The Gospel provides us with an attractive portrait of him, recording his words: "Let us go too and die with him" (Jn 11:16) and "Lord, we do not know where you are going, so how can we know the way? (Jn 14:5) and Jesus' words to him: "Happy are those who have not seen and yet believe" (Jn 20:29).

Readings: Eph 2:19–22
Ps 117
Jn 20:24–29

6 *Maria Goretti.* In 1902 at Nettuno, this young girl of twelve, the eldest of six children and in charge of the family at home because her mother, a widow, had to go out to work, was stabbed by a young man of eighteen who desired her. Later, at her canonization, he was present.

7 *Benedict.* The father of Western monasticism and the patron saint of Europe was a student at Rome when he decided to seek solitude at Subiaco. There a community grew up around him and he later moved to Monte Cassino. He wrote a rule for his monastic communities which is a finely balanced model of respect for human possibilities. Everything is moderation in the Benedictine way of life, which is based on work and prayer, community life and vigilance on the part of the abbot. Since the founder's death in 547, Benedictine monasticism has given the world a soul and the Church a constant source of life and hope.

22 *Mary Magdalene.* The anonymous sinner in Luke's Gospel who anointed Jesus' feet with perfume (Lk 7:36ff), Mary of Bethany, who listened to him (Lk 10:38ff) and sent for him when her brother Lazarus

was dying (Jn 11:1ff), and a little later anointed him as a sign of his burial (Jn 12:1ff), and finally Mary of Magdala, who recognized the risen Christ on Easter morning (Jn 20:11ff, the Gospel for today's feast)—should they all be seen as one person? There is no real need to, nor is there any need to weigh Mary down with all the sins of the world in order to make her presence on Easter morning even more wonderful. But whether it is many different women or only one, the cult of Mary Magdalene has long been popular in the West.

25 *James the Great.* Whether you believe in the legend or not, you will never prevent Spain from venerating Saint James as its patron saint. For centuries, pilgrims have come from every part of the world to Santiago de Compostela, the city of Saint James, the Matamore or "killer of the Moors," whose body, it is thought, was brought to Galicia and who is believed to have led the reconquest of Christian Spain. What is the reason for this pilgrimage? Is it just because a call from the "ends of the earth" has always reached men's hearts? Or is it rather because of the importance of the apostle James himself, whom Christ called a "son of thunder"? With Peter and John, he witnessed the Lord's transfiguration and his final suffering. He was also put to death by Herod's men at Jerusalem, where he seems to have played a very important part.

Readings: 2 Cor 4:7–15
Ps 126
Mt 20:20–28

26 *Anna and Joachim.* We know little about Mary's parents apart from their very meaningful names: "Full of grace'" and "Yahweh has established." And yet they have their place in history.

29 *Martha.* We should not simply dismiss her because she did the housework while her sister meditated on the word (Lk 10:38–42). Hospitality and making guests welcome are great virtues, although the simplest welcomes are always the best, those which are not lost in numerous little anxieties. Did the evangelist want to restore Martha to her rightful position? After all, he tells us that it was she who confessed in a very striking way the fundamental Christian conviction: "I believe that you are the Christ, the Son of God, the one who was to come in to this world" (Jn 11:19–27: the raising of Lazarus).

31 *Ignatius of Loyola.* He was a soldier, used to conquest. Basque blood ran in his veins. Much of his life was spent at the court of the King of Navarre. Then he was wounded at the siege of Pampeluna and spent a year in a cave at Manresa. At Montserrat he made a vow to dedicate himself to Christ. In Jerusalem he was overcome with passion for Jesus. He studied and was regarded by some as one of the Illuminati. He went to Paris and, when he was forty-three, he, Francis Xavier and several others made a vow to go to Palestine. He was ordained in Venice and Pope Paul III entrusted the little group of men with mission work in Italy. Finally, he set up a new order in the Church: the Company of Jesus. The Jesuits were always intended to form an elite group closely linked to the Pope—even though one Pope in the eighteenth century, Clement XIV, suppressed them. They are still filled with great zeal for Christ and nowadays many of them want to work in areas where people are treated unjustly. St. Ignatius' *Spiritual Exercises,* begun at Manresa and completed in Paris, are still valuable reading for the apostolic conversion of those who already believe—a conversion "to the greater glory of God."

AUGUST

1 *Alphonsus Liguori.* During the age of the Enlightenment and just before the French Revolution, this Italian aristocrat who practiced as a lawyer in Naples became a priest and devoted himself to work among the poor. He founded the Congregation of the Most Holy Redeemer with a group of other priests ("Redemptorists"). In his writings especially, he attacked the arid teachings of the Jansenists.

4 *Jean-Baptiste Marie Vianney.* Even at the time of the French Revolution, this man of peasant stock listened to the voice of reason and, in spite of everything, became a priest. For forty-two years he remained the Cure of Ars. There was no glory in his mission, but in certain years as many as a hundred thousand people came to confess to him. He was a contemplative, at home with the supernatural, a man of God who believed with all his heart in his ministry. He is the patron saint of parish priests.

5 *The Dedication of the Church of Santa Maria Maggiore.* This church was the first in the West to be dedicated to the Virgin Mary. The event took place just before the Council of Ephesus. (See January 1).

6 *The Transfiguration of the Lord.*

> Readings: Dan 7:9–10, 13–14 or 2 Pet 1:16–19
> Ps 97
> Mt 17:1–9 (Year A) or Mk 9:2–10 (Year B) or LK 9:28b–36 (Year C)

He took them aside at the top of a mountain. He told them to stand aside, far away from the muddy paths, and contemplate the horizon. To stand aside, away from the noisy world, and listen to the appeal made by God from on high. To stand aside, close to God, and then, after a while, to go down again to live close to men's hearts. His face became like fire and his clothes as white as light—the face of a man to whom God has shown himself and a cloak of joy wrapping the body of the beloved Son to be handed over too soon to death. At the summit of the mountain, the tired men contemplated the face that no one could see without dying. A cloud of peace covered them with its shadow and then parted. God said: "This is my Son." God's words are those of a father. They are suddenly afraid and fall on their faces on the ground, listening to the words that come from beyond. They hear the voice of the Father who is bending over them in their wretchedness, ready to give them back the life they have lost in that garden, where man tried to rise up against him. "Where are you, Adam?" (Gn 3:9). Stand up, poor man made of dust! The Son of Man is looking at you. Forget your self-satisfaction and contemplate Jesus, in whom God wants to begin again for you—going as far as the cross and the garden of Easter, when everything will be transfigured.

7 *Juliana of Liège.* She was born near Liège in 1192 and was orphaned when she was very young and brought up by the beguines who looked after the leper hospital of Mont-Cornillon at the city gates. She was given a good education, well suited to her lively and inquiring mind. She became a beguine herself and was eventually appointed to the position of prioress. In an attempt to make her sisters more committed, she took over the administration of the leper hospital from the commune, but incurred such hostility that she had to go first to Salzinnes, then to Namur and finally to Fosses, which was subject to the suzerainty of Liège. It was there that she died in 1258 and it was also there that the feast of Corpus Christi was celebrated for the first

time in 1246, thanks to the bishop, Robert de Thourotte and to the efforts of Juliana, who had been trying since 1208 to have this new feast celebrated. Pope Urban IV, the son of a shoemaker from Troyes and at one time archdeacon of Fosses, extended its celebration in 1264 to the universal Church.

8 *Dominic.* Born in Old Castile, Dominic became aware of the unhappy state of Languedoc caused by the Cathari during an apostolic journey with his bishop, Diego, which took him to Denmark. With the consent of Pope Innocent III, he stayed in the region of Narbonne and Toulouse to evangelize those "new towns" in which the feudally minded clergy could offer no alternative to the fervent and poor way of life led by the heretical Cathari. Dominic preached poverty and lived as a poor man, but his difficult ministry was unfortunately not furthered by the Albigensian Crusade launched against the heretics by the king and the Pope and ending in bloodshed and cruelty. In the meantime, however, he had succeeded in converting some Albigensian women at Prouille and had founded the Dominican Order. After recognition by the Fourth Lateran Council in 1215, he was given a preaching mission by the bishop of Toulouse and established the bases of the Order of Preachers, whose members were to follow the rule of St. Augustine, but live evangelically in Paris, Bologna and Madrid, and other restless and energetic cities. By the time he was fifty-one, he was exhausted and he died in Bologna in 1221.

10 *Lawrence.* He was Pope Sixtus II's deacon. During Valerian's persecution of the Church, he refused to hand the archives and the lists of the Church's possessions to the authorities. Later on, the third of Rome's great basilicas was dedicated to him and he was venerated there, with Peter and Paul, as the city's protector.

11 *Clare.* She was only nineteen when, overpowered with love for Lady Poverty, she went to the Portiuncula on Palm Sunday to join Francis, who had also left Assisi. She became the abbess of the "Poor Ladies" at San Damiano, where she in turn received Francis just before his death. There, the exhausted Poverello was able to rest and praise God for all his creatures and for "our Sister Death." The "Canticle of All Creatures" was probably written or at least completed at San Damiano.

15 *The Assumption of the Virgin Mary.*

Readings: Vigil: 1 Chr 15:3–4, 15–16; 16:1–2
Ps 132
1 Cor 15:54–57
Lk 11:27–28
Day: Rv 11:19a; 12:1–6a, 10ab
Ps 45
1 Cor 15:20–26
Lk 1:39–56

"A great sign appeared in heaven: a woman adorned with the sun . . ." pregnant and in labor in order to set life free. A mother—the mother of men. A woman, clothed in the garment of transfiguration. And, opposite her, death, watching and waiting, a cunning dragon, red like fire, ready to devour her child.

What a powerful sense of life and death emerges from the Book of Revelation! Raising our eyes to heaven, we see how our infinitely small planet, earth, is reflected in the light of what is infinitely great. A birth in the obscurity of Bethlehem is the sign given to men so that they will understand the meaning of their history. And Mary, that obscure woman, becomes for us a word of God and a revelation of his grace.

Would it have been possible for God to abandon that woman and that man to the power of death? To nothingness, the void without a future? Did woman have to be forever the sign of desire, lost blood and endlessly repeated death? Did man and woman have always to be born and give birth in pain and the child tremble in its mother's womb to nourish the demon and death? No! "A great sign has appeared in heaven: a woman adorned with the sun." That sign is Mary, in whom every woman can recognize her grace and her vocation—Mary who gives birth to life which is the light of a dawn without end. She is the sign of life among us.

Cursed be the woman who is no longer clothed in the sun, which is the garment of virginity of the heart and the spirit. Blessed be the woman who hands herself over entirely to life and to God. But giving birth is always painful and always calls for patience. The woman's child is taken from her, taken for another kind of glory, and the woman goes into the desert—our desert. Mary is with us in this desert in which life and death, love and pride and fear and freedom are struggling against each other in a battle in which our resurrection is born. Our earth has been closely acquainted with pain since its creation and everything in us calls out for God. Let us be bold enough and say that Mary is in heaven in her motherhood, since every human being is called to God with and in his or her own body.

No, woman in the flesh is not a symbol of death. Woman has found in Mary her icon of great beauty, an image that will not be taken away from her. But it is in the desert that that beauty is able to express itself openly, without fear of being possessed by the cunning of the enemy. The dawn is more beautiful in the desert than anywhere else. The desert of Easter—the dawn of Easter! It was then that the Son, reborn, could say to his mother: "Woman, come with me! I will wrap your pain in a garment of love."

20 *Bernard.* Citeaux, Burgundy, 1112—a twenty-two year old nobleman had just knocked at the door of the poor monastery of Stephen Harding. With him were thirty friends and members of his family who wanted to be monks and live a life of poverty. The young man's name was Bernard. He was to devote his fiery spirit, his mystical soul and his passion for the Church to Citeaux. A few years later he founded Clairvaux, which became immensely successful. The Cistercian Order quickly spread throughout Europe. Bernard was active everywhere in defense of the Church. He combatted Abelard's rationalism, the civil disturbances caused by Arnold of Brescia and the ambiguous and false teachings of the Cathari. He supported the Pope in his struggle against secular power in Rome and Liège. He helped the noblemen and leaders at Vézelay to launch the Second Crusade. At the same time, he often returned to Clairvaux to supervise the lives of his monks and to preach to them. He has been called the last of the Church Fathers. He may, it is true, not have been very open to scientific knowledge, but he had a warm heart and a solid faith. His Commentary on the Song of Songs is well worth reading.

21 *Pius X.* This Pope, who died at the time of the outbreak of the First World War, is reputed to have remained a country priest at heart. His personal holiness is reflected in the reforms that are still bearing fruit today in the liturgy and sacramental life. He above all encouraged frequent Communion. He was less successful in his struggle against Christian democracy in Italy and France, which he was hardly able to understand, although he supported the movement in Belgium and Austria, countries which were more submissive to the episcopate. He

was less fortunate too in his condemnation of modernism, which consisted of a blend of sensitivity to historical and exegetical criticism and a rationalism that was undoubtedly harmful to faith.

23 *Rose of Lima.* Living in a materialistic colonial society, that of South America, this humble Dominican tertiary was a model of holiness, charm and self-denial.

24 *Bartholomew.* This unobtrusive apostle, who is probably the same as Nathanael (see the Gospel of the day), shows us how a stubborn but loyal man can become a very effective witness to the faith.

Readings: Acts 21:9b–14
Ps 145
Jn 1:45–51

25 *Louis IX.* Very few kings have been saints, but if St. Louis had been the only one, that would have been quite enough. He was indisputably a holy king, and his just treatment of his humble subjects is not simply legendary. He was also an exemplary husband and a good father of eleven children. He was a simple and approachable man and a leader who refused to wage war to increase his own territory while harming the enemy. In a word, he was a saint. Inspired by the ideal of knighthood, he went on two crusades, dying during the second at Tunis in 1270. He was, then, the last of the crusaders.

27 *Monica.* Saint Augustine's mother. See below.

28 *Augustine.* He was born at Tagaste in North Africa in 354. His mother, Monica, was a Christian and his father was a Roman public servant who made great sacrifices to find the right situation for his son. He was enrolled among the catechumens when he was born, but his baptism was delayed again and again. His adolescence was stormy. When he was only eighteen, he had a son, Adeodatus, by a mistress to whom he remained faithful for fourteen years. This did not prevent him from studying, and by the time he was twenty he was already teaching rhetoric at Carthage. He still did not know how to order his life and was for some time tempted by Manichaeism, because he was troubled by the problem of evil. His mother longed for him to become a Christian. His father died baptized. When he was thirty he went with Monica to Milan, where he taught philosophy. There he was influenced

not only by neo-Platonism, but also by the Gospels. He was also personally influenced by Ambrose, the bishop of Milan. One day, when he was thirty-two, he heard the voice of a child telling him: "Tolle, lege," and, opening the Bible, he was filled with light. He was baptized with his son on Easter night 387. That same year, his mother died at Ostia. Two years later, Adeodatus also died. Augustine went back to Tagaste and led a religious life there with friends. He became a priest at Hippo and soon became famous as a preacher, although he had not been consecrated as a bishop. He became a bishop in 395 and for the next thirty-four years was the leading religious and theological thinker in the Church. It would hardly be an exaggeration to claim that he has continued to be that ever since. He writes as a pastor of souls, but also polemically, in his eagerness to correct errors and deviations from true faith. There were many false teachers during his life—Manichaeans, Donatists, and Pelagians, who were almost Stoics. In opposition to their teaching, Augustine stressed grace and the gratuitous nature of salvation. At the same time, however, he also emphasized man's sinfulness so much that future "Augustinians" such as Luther were marked by deep pessimism. Augustine also experienced the coming of the Vandals and the eclipse of Rome by the Barbarians. His great work *The City of God* is an attempt on a grandiose scale to understand world history in the light of faith—a faith that was not extinguished even when the world was changing.

> Late have I loved you, beauty so old and so new. You were within me and I was outside myself. And it was there that I was looking for you. You called me. You cried out and came to the limit of my deafness. You touched me and I am burning with longing for your peace (*The Confessions*).

29 *The Martyrdom of John the Baptist.*

> Gospel: Mk 6:17–29
> (See the Friday of the Fourth Week of Ordinary Time)

SEPTEMBER
3 *Gregory the Great.* He was prefect of Rome in the mid-sixth century and continued to hold this office in a sense when he became Pope,

after having been a monk and legate in Constantinople. Frightened by the Lombard invasions, the people of Rome trusted him and he proved to be an excellent administrator of the Church. He was able to bring his dialogue with the Lombards to a satisfactory conclusion, he encouraged the Franks, he provided a firm foundation for papal power, and he sent an apostolic mission to convert England (see May 27). As Pope, he called himself the "servant of the servants of God." The link between his name and Gregorian chant is largely imaginary, because, if Gregory favored any liturgy, he would have used the "Old Roman" chant, which disappeared in the fourteenth century.

8 *The Birth of the Virgin Mary.* This feast of Mary was originally connected with the dedication of a church in Jerusalem, where Anna's house was situated according to tradition.

Readings: Mi 5:1–4a or Rom 8:28–30
           Ps 13
           Mt 1:1–16, 18–23

See the commentary for December 17.

13 *John Chrysostom.* He was a monk and his health was not good. He became a priest at Antioch and later patriarch of Constantinople. No one could prevent him from defending the cause of less fortunate people, and this brought him into disfavor with Empress Eudoxia. He was exiled and a close watch was kept on him. He was then sent to a more remote place in the foothills of the Caucasus, but on the way there—a journey of a thousand miles—he died. He was greatly loved and his eloquence earned him the name of "Golden Mouth" (Chrysostomos). In addition to his immense literary output, he was also responsible for much of the Orthodox liturgy, which he made into the prayer of the poor who have no other heaven on earth but the Church.

14 *The Glorious Cross of the Lord.*

Readings: Nm 21:4b–9 or Phil 2:6–11
           Ps 78
           Jn 3:13–17

The desert—the burning, biting sun and the scorching sky and skeletons, bearing witness to death. The place where men are forgotten. Very rarely is it a place that attracts men—an oasis. Very often it is a place where they complain and criticize—the desert of life. People die not only of cancer, leukemia and coronary thrombosis, but also because they simply do not know where they are going. They may still have the strength to raise their eyes, but all they see are serpents that bite them to death.

But God knows. He knows all the more because his Son died forsaken in the desert, outside the walls of the city. We now believe—and especially on this day—that the cross is glorious. But at the time a curse hung over the one who was dying, nailed to the wood. Was God the origin of that curse? Many people thought so. Sooner or later we all come to recognize that death is the last fatal injury or that it is an ineradicable patch of leprosy gradually spreading and for a long time confused with a beauty spot. The words of the prophet were applied to Christ: "Without beauty, without majesty we saw him" (Is 53:2). He is united with all those who lower their heads in a gesture that will one day put an end to their lives when death is victorious over them. And who would blame us for complaining?

Yet the cross is still glorious. It is a cross raised up above the world. The old serpent has taken on the face of man, and God, coming down to us in his Son who emptied himself totally, has raised the cross far above our wretchedness. The bite of death has been transfigured into a source of life. The cross is glorious because, from that time onward, the face of suffering man has shone with the love of God.

In the desert of the world, we have the task of raising up a sign of the future that is stronger than death. That is not just a question of setting up crucifixes everywhere. It means that we ourselves have to be so marked by love that everyone can recognize the face of Christ and be conscious of the hope of healing. The caduceus of the medical profession, Hermes' rod with its entwined serpents, is also a sign of healing, but in the end the only treatment that can save man is one that combines love and scientific knowledge. In the desert of man, people struggle against death so that those who are weak, handicapped and incurable may live more human lives and death is driven back, even though we know that we shall never overcome it completely. Yet death is always overcome whenever love prevents it from reigning over us.

16 *Cornelius and Cyprian.* A converted lawyer, Cyprian became the bishop of Carthage. He had no real enemies. He engaged in vehement controversy with Pope Stephen, who was more flexible than he was, on the difficult question of the readmission to Church membership of Christians baptized by heretics. Cyprian was so attached to the Church that he could not accept the presence of the Church unless there was pure faith. But his attention was soon turned toward more urgent matters when the Church once again became persecuted. He helped the exiled Pope Cornelius during his last days on earth and died a martyr's death himself in 258 A.D.

21 *Matthew.* See Volume II.

22 *Maurice and his Companions.* These Roman soldiers, who were martyred because they refused to put Christians to death, are honored in Switzerland. Although a whole legion of soldiers was probably not involved, there is firm evidence that the event took place.

27 *Vincent de Paul.* He was a great saint in a great century. Vincent gave an evangelical flavor, which is all too often lacking from human history, to the seventeenth century. Born a peasant in the southwest of France, he became a priest and very quickly came into contact with the leaders of France at the time. He knew Cardinal Bérulle and Francis de Sales and others, and Louis XIII died in his arms. But he also became aware of the misery of the poor, the galley prisoners, and the uneducated rural workers. He was a brilliant organizer and initiated at least two movements—the Sisters of Charity, with Louise de Marillac, and the Congregation of the Mission or Lazarists. He also reformed seminaries in the conviction that only deeply evangelical clergy could make the Church truly present in the world. The Society of Vincent de Paul extended this spirit to lay people in the nineteenth century.

29 *Michael, Raphael and Gabriel.* "Who is like God?"—"God heals"—"God is strong." The cult of the angels is directed toward God and the names of the angels are expressions of God. The liturgy associates us with their praise and unites us with their mission. When he wanted to come to us, God sent his angels. But who can ever say what they really

are? Should we not be satisfied with the knowledge that God's heaven is populated with myriads of beings and that the way between heaven and earth is covered by these messengers?

Readings: Dn 7:9–10, 13–14 or Rv 12:7–12a
Ps 138
Jn 1:47–51

30 *Jerome.* He was born in Dalmatia, but went to Rome, full of enthusiasm for Scripture. Later in life he settled in Bethlehem. Throughout the whole of his life, he worked at a translation of and a commentary on the Bible. A man of difficult temperament, he died in 420 A.D.

OCTOBER

1 *Theresa of the Infant Jesus.* It would be quite wrong to think of the "little Saint Theresa" as a pampered child who became a Carmelite because of her extremely religious family background. That is true, but it is not the full story. She was a self-willed young woman and life was hard in the Carmel of Lisieux. She had long periods of spiritual aridity which brought her frequently very close to atheism of a kind that is very familiar to us today. She was deeply in communion with the world and fully deserves to be called the "patron saint of missions." It is true too that she summed up the whole of her life in the "little way" and in love as the "most perfect way," but she paid a high price for the love that she experienced. Her message has been made very well known by the publication of her *Autobiography of a Saint* and it has brought countless people who had been made anxious and unhappy by religion to God. That is the greatest grace that Theresa has mediated to our century. She died in 1897 with these words on her lips: "Everything is grace!"

> This year God has given me the grace to know what charity is. I have always known that charity should not remain enclosed in the depths of the heart. "No one," Jesus told us, "lights a lamp to put it under a tub; they put it on a lampstand, where it shines for everyone in the house." It

seems to me that the lamp represents charity, which must light the house and make everyone, without any exceptions, in the house happy.

4 *Francis of Assisi.* He might have become a rich merchant like his father or a knight, as he was for a while when he was very young, or simply a hermit, as he was at St. Mary of the Angels between the ages of seventeen and twenty. But he became a poor man, taking poverty to the peak of glory, making poverty his bride and raising it to the level of a rule of life for his brethren. He took the evangelical call to poverty more seriously than perhaps any Christian in history and reinterpreted almost everything for the Church and the world, which was passing through a period of deep change. He did not make his brethren monks, too closely tied to the feudal system, or priests, too closely tied to their status, but beggars! As mendicant friars, they were as poor as the beaten path as they went from village to village begging their keep, with Christ and the Gospel as their only model, and as free as the birds of the air. Francis had to be both patient and determined to have his plan recognized, but eventually Popes Innocent III and Honorius III approved it, although it met with little enthusiasm among the bishops. But the Church received the great gift from God of a poet who praised the sun and the whole of creation in a canticle that the little poor man of Assisi composed when he was almost blind and near the end of his life on earth. Francis also spoke intimately to the hearts of the most simple believers when he bore in his own body the signs of Christ's suffering. He died in 1126 at Assisi. People still visit the town in great numbers and breathe there the perfume of "true and perfect joy," possibly less in the great basilica built over his tomb than in the humble church of San Damiano.

6 *Bruno.* A canon at Cologne and later at Rheims, he taught Pope Urban II. Inspired by the ideals of Cluny, he went in 1083 to consult Robert of Molesmes, who later founded Citeaux. Robert sent Bruno into the mountainous regions known as the Chartreuse near Grenoble, where he founded the Carthusian Order, the members of which lead a monastic life based on eremitism.

9 *Dionysius and His Companions.* Certain facts of Dionysius' life are regarded as historically established: he was the first bishop of Paris, he was martyred with his companions on the "Mount of Martyrs"

(Montmartre), and he was buried where the Benedictine Abbey of Saint Denis was built in the seventh century. He himself lived and died in the third century. We cannot be so sure about the departure of the missionaries for Rome or about his identification with Dionysius the Areopagite, converted by Paul in Athens. This legend was strongly disputed in the seventeenth century and by Abelard, but it is featured in most of the illustrations of the life of Dionysius of Paris.

15 *Teresa of Avila.* This woman was on fire with the spirit of Castilian chivalry. At eighteen, she entered a lax Carmelite convent without any strong sense of vocation. Years later, she experienced an inner reform that was so profound that she was transported to the peak of mystical love. At the age of forty-five, she began her work of reforming Carmelite spirituality, traveling all over Spain and overcoming all obstacles. She lived from 1515 to 1582.

17 *Ignatius of Antioch.* Ignatius, the bishop of Antioch in Syria, lived during the apostolic period. He was taken to Rome, where he died as a martyr in 177 A.D. On the way, he wrote letters to the churches he visited. His insistence on the unity of the Church shows how much resistance he encountered.

> Do nothing apart from the bishop and the priests. Do not imagine that you can do anything good apart from them. The only good that you can do is in common with them.

18 *Luke.* See Volume III.

19 *John de Brébeuf and Isaac Jogues,* French Jesuits, apostles of Quebec. They were killed by Indians in 1646 and 1649.

28 *Simon and Jude.* Little is said about these two apostles in the Gospels. Simon, called the Zealot, must have been a member of one of those groups of violent men who worked underground for the restoration of the kingdom of Israel. The same concern can be detected in Jude, who asked Jesus: "Do you intend to show yourself to us and not to the world" (Jn 14:22). Both men had to learn that the way to the kingdom of God was "not of this world."

Readings: Eph 2:19–22
Ps 19a
Lk 6:12–19

NOVEMBER
1 *All Saints.*

Readings: Rv 7:2–4, 9–14
Ps 24
1 Jn 3:1–3
Mt 5:1–12a

Two groups of people, very different from each other and yet very similar, are brought together today. On the one hand, there are the many humble people who have followed Jesus, hardly believing that they are what he called blessed, when everything seems to have conspired to oppress them. On the other hand, there are those who have followed him to death and beyond, convinced of their own happiness. Neither of these groups has anything in common with those who are disappointed in their pursuit of a false holiness or with the dismal platitudes we read on tombstones. But both have this in common with each other—well known or obscure, they are true saints.

All saints are in some way quite new and special. None of them was born perfect, of course, but all of them have believed that God is new and special, particularly in promising his kingdom to the poor and humble. The saints are new and special men and women who have gone, as it were, in the opposite direction, because Christ, in proclaiming the Beatitudes, wanted to set the world going in the opposite direction.

There are, then, the famous saints and those who have to wait a long time to be canonized. But does it really matter? God loves them and they are holy because they have believed in his love. Going against the grain, they have rediscovered love and have borne witness to a new world. We hardly speak at all about them, but God thanks them in his eternity. Surely that is what holiness is: God thanking you for having believed in him.

These men and women are blessed indeed. They are happy because they have forgiven others without a trace of resentment, have not listened to self-justification and have smiled on the darkest of mornings. Their hearts are pure. The window panes through which they look have not been made dirty by the polluted air of the world in which they live. There is no need to say: "I am no saint," because God only wants to give us his holiness, and it is better to let him go ahead, since we are so clumsy. Let us be aware of the love with which God loves us and offer no resistance to him. Holiness can be seen on people's faces—it is transparent and overflowing with the peace that comes from the heart. "When what we are to be in the future has been revealed, we shall be like him, because we shall see him as he really is" (1 Jn 3:2). Holiness is this: tell me at whom you are looking and I will tell you what your holiness is. But how many people are disappointed, because they are only looking at themselves. Look at Christ and you will be holy. Look at him and let yourself be led by him.

2 *All Souls*. We all have encountered death. And you encounter it every day if your eyes are open, because it is there, at the very heart of your life. You are older today than you were yesterday. Disappointment grips your flesh. Your children are dreaming of a world that will not be your world. The names of death are: divorce, war, solitude, children without parents and parents without children. The earth is half hidden behind a veil of mourning. It is like a mist. Tomorrow our graveyards will once again be sleeping under faded chrysanthemums.

We all have encountered death and we have followed it. It is not always terrible. It can be attractive. Which one of us has never called on death during an endless night? We have followed death because it has followed us since the day we were born, and we have sometimes thought of asking it: "Go ahead of us—you know where we are going." We have, it is true, shed tears of mourning, but we have always known that this world is a vale of tears.

But we have also encountered Christ—the one who so many said was dead. The day we encountered death, we encountered him. We had to go down to the deepest pit of our solitude to feel his hand resting on us, his eyes looking at us and his great age reviving our youth. We encountered the one who is alive and he told us: "Follow me! I know death very well and I will let you see its other face."

We had often been told about him. His Church has always joyfully proclaimed his resurrection. But for us they were mere words—until the day that we encountered death with him. He led us to a table. He gave us brothers—his disciples who ran away to die in their own country while he was stretched out in solitude on the cross. He offered us the cup and invited us to drink from it with him. He told us: "Share this with your brothers and go on the way with my disciples."

We have encountered death—the death of Jesus Christ—and we have known life. We have shared the death of our fellow men and we have tasted hope. We have accepted our death and we have very gently tamed it. We have told death: "You are our bride!" But it was not the faded death of our graveyards. It was death that had been conquered, the death of the garden in springtime and the open tomb, death in which men had buried the Lord without knowing that he would, on the Sunday morning, make the lily of the valley flower on our graves and let the scent of a sprig of lavender fill our solitude.

If you have your eyes open and encounter—today or tomorrow—a man, a woman, a child or an old person whose eyes reflect death, listen to the voice asking you to share his or her suffering in the name of Jesus Christ. And let fall into that person's heart a little drop of that blood that you have received at the table of life. Then death will be conquered even if everything still seems to be dying.

4 *Charles Borromeo*. This great archbishop of Milan, who was a model for the Church of the Council of Trent, was converted late in life. He was the nephew of Pius IV and a doctor of law. He was made a cardinal and the administrator of Milan at the age of twenty-two, but without thinking it necessary to become a priest. He played a prominent part in the last sessions of the Council and was not ordained a priest and consecrated a bishop until it was over. Then he began to work energetically to reform the Church, making pastoral visits, holding diocesan synods, creating seminaries and encouraging catechetical work.

7 *Willibrord* was a companion of Boniface (see June 5) and, like him, an English monk. He evangelized Frisia, Flanders and Germany. He became the bishop of Utrecht and founded the Abbey of Echternach, where he died in 739. He was helped in his work by Pepin and Charles Martel.

9 *Dedication of the Lateran Basilica*. The papal cathedral is built on a domain of the Laterani family which was given to the Church by Constantine. The Popes lived at the Lateran until the end of the Middle Ages. The celebration of this dedication affirms the close ties between the whole Church and the "mother and head of all the churches."

Readings: Ez 47:1–2, 8–9, 12 or 1 Cor 3:9b–11, 16–17
Ps 46
Jn 2:13–22

10 *Leo the Great.* During the period when the Huns and Vandals were sweeping through Italy and even into Rome, Pope Leo, who was originally a Roman himself, appeared as a great leader. He intervened with the barbarians and, even more importantly, took part in theological discussions in matters that deeply concerned the East and impressed the Council of Chalcedon (451 A.D.) with his authority (see January 1).

11 *Martin of Tours.* This Roman soldier, a native of Pannonia, one day shared his cloak with a beggar. This was a sign of grace—a grace that did not prevent him from being called the "peasant from the Danube." He was ordained by Hilary of Poitiers, founded the first monastery in Gaul, and thus introduced the monastic way of life into the region. In 371 A.D. he became bishop of Tours and organized rural parishes and set up other monasteries in his diocese. He was criticized by many less zealous bishops, but his Christian achievement was very great. After his death, Tours became a center of pilgrimage and many churches are dedicated to him.

15 *Albert the Great.* A German Dominican who also taught at Paris and was Thomas Aquinas' master at Cologne, he had an unusually open mind and worked hard to make the writings of and based on Aristotle known and to show their compatibility with faith. He gave a great impetus to profane studies in the Middle Ages.

22 *Cecilia.* This Roman saint is very popular, but nothing that can be accepted as authentic is known about her. She is the patron saint of musicians, because, according to a legend, she "sang in her heart for God" on her wedding day.

23 *Andrew.* Andrew was venerated in Constantinople as Peter is in Rome. He is also the patron saint of Russia and Scotland. Before he followed Jesus, he was a disciple of John the Baptist. In the Gospels, it is often Andrew who introduces the others to Christ.

Readings: Rom 10:9–18
Ps 19a
Mt 4:18–22

DECEMBER

3 *Francis Xavier.* He was a companion of Ignatius Loyola (see July 31). He evangelized Goa, Malacca, the Molucca Islands and Japan. He died on the way to China in 1552. He is the patron saint of missions.

6 *Nicholas.* All that can be said with certainty about Nicholas is that he was the bishop of Myra in Lycia, Asia Minor. According to legend, the three daughters of a neighbor who had resorted to prostitution to avoid penury were saved by his generosity. Partly because of this legend, he became the patron saint of good children in Greece, Russia, England and northern Europe.

7 *Ambrose.* He was only a catechumen when the people of Milan called for him to be their bishop. At that time he was the provincial consul of the district and had achieved peace for the city. As bishop, he was able to hold his own against the power of the emperor and even went so far as to excommunicate Theodosius for a long time because of the latter's massacre at Thessalonica in 390 A.D. He was an intelligent and cultured man who wrote extensively. His liturgical writings, including hymns and psalms, are influenced by Eastern models. He died in 397.

8 *The Immaculate Conception of the Virgin Mary.*

Readings: Gen 3:9–15, 20
   Ps 98
   Eph 1:3–6, 11–12
   Lk 1:26–38

"Blessed be God! In Jesus, he has chosen us before the creation of the world, so that we might be in love holy and blameless in his sight." When the Church turns to Mary to tell her, echoing the words of the Annunciation and the Visitation: "You are full of grace and you are blessed," it is in fact looking at an icon of itself, and all who belong to it can find in the woman who was "of all women the most blessed" (Lk 1:42) the vocation to which he or she has been called by God.

In the garden of Genesis, the man and the woman hid themselves from God. They were suddenly ashamed of having wanted to do without him. Everything had at the same time suddenly begun to deteriorate. Death had entered the world and human life seemed to be becoming extinguished in a tide of evil. But a promise had been given to man—

the woman was called Eve, "Life," the mother of living men. Death was not the last word. But sin still had to be overcome if life was to be born again.

God's plan was fulfilled, after Eve, in Mary. A woman was given to us in her who is blessed, holy and full of grace. The Lord our God, Emmanuel, is with her. He is so much with her that he was born of her and has worked closely with her to save man. Salvation comes to us from the Mother of the living who, in order to give man hope for the future, began by bearing within her and giving birth to the Son of God. Mary's grace is called Jesus. There is no distance separating our Savior from his Mother. She was at the cross with him. She is also glorified with him. And she leads us to him.

Mary is immaculate—unspotted by sin. That is not an exception in God's plan. It is the proclamation of every human vocation. Mary is unspotted and beautiful so that all of us may be called to be beautiful and have a taste for beauty. She is the mother of all men so that all men may cease to listen to that insidious voice that calls them away from God and listen to her. Listening to Mary is going with her to the source of grace—her Son, who was born of her because she said "yes" unreservedly to God. Mary teaches us to say "yes" to God and in so doing gives birth to holiness in us. She gives us her Son as only a mother can.

Yes—blessed be God! And blessed be his loving kindness! The Mother of the living is also blessed because through her we can receive life without fearing that it may lead to death. The man or woman who lives in holiness has overcome death with Christ.

13 *Lucy.* Nothing is known about this martyr from Syracuse. Her name reminds us of light and she has been venerated in many places since the fifth century.

14 *John of the Cross.* Meeting Teresa of Avila made this disheartened Carmelite undertake the task of reforming his order. He encountered great opposition and was even imprisoned for several months. He was isolated for the rest of his life, but, despite this hostility, he wrote impressively beautiful lyrical and mystical works.

> I know the spring that rises and flows away,
> but it is night.

Though this eternal spring is hidden,
I have found it—
but it is night.

In the dark night of this exile here
I know the cool spring by faith,
but it is night.

I do not know its source, for it has none,
but know that every source flows from it—
but it is night.

I know no thing as beautiful
and by it the thirst of heaven and earth is quenched,
but it is night.

It calls out to every creature
whose thirst is quenched by this water darkly,
but it is night.

I long to be invited to this source of living water—
I see it in this bread of life.
But it is night.